# Fighting Patriots

## The First Three Years Of
## Homewood High School Football

ISBN: 978-1-09830-517-8

# TABLE OF CONTENTS

# Fighting Patriots

## The First Three Years Of Homewood High School Football

## By Patrick Kirk

Edited by Anne Hill Henders and Lisa Hodgens

Cover Design by Shawn Wright

# FORWARD

This book is dedicated to the exceptional citizens of the city of Homewood. Their commitment to a better education for their children laid the foundation for the creation of the Homewood School System in 1970 and, with it, the outstanding high school.

It took a combined effort of all the people of this wonderful city to launch the vibrant and well-planned educational system. From academics to athletics, arts to extracurricular activities, Homewood High School has been recognized for its standard of excellence and these accolades continue to this day.

I am privileged and honored to have been part of this distinguished school system.

**Michael S. Gross**

Homewood City School System (1965-1985)

Superintendent, Principal, Assistant Principal, and Teacher

# INTRODUCTION

There were a few seconds left on the clock in the fourth quarter of the 1974 4A State Championship game at Legion Field. This was enough time for one more play. One more pass to the end zone for Dothan to score and win by three. Steadman Shealy dropped back to the forty yard line and let the ball fly. Dothan's best player, Greg Ramsey, their running back who had scored on a 70 yard run in the first half, had come out of the backfield, sprinted down the east side of the field into the end zone. The ball was a beautifully thrown pass to the corner of the end zone where no one but the Dothan running back was within reach of the ball. He extended his arms fully and the wet ball slid off his frozen hand in slow motion as the Homewood players, coaches and fans held their breath for the last play to end in their favor. Time on the clock ran out and the scoreboard remained Homewood 10 Dothan 7 in the final game of the 1974 season. This is how it ended for the seniors who played for the twenty-six year old Coach Alvin Bresler; the youngest coach to win an Alabama State Championship, a few of them on all three of his Homewood Patriot teams. How it began, and what happened in between is a story worth telling.

**"A Community of Champions"Homewood's 'Fighting Patriots'**
**March to Victory** *by Todd Foreman (HHS Class of 1976)*

*Opening*

When Patrick Kirk called and asked me to help write the grand story of a very young and very successful Coach Alvin Bresler, I felt honored but also reticent, as I didn't feel that I had much to contribute. Though I had been a leader in Homewood High School during his coaching years, I didn't have a lot of personal contact with him.

But like the rest of our small, tight-knit community, I loved to watch his Patriot Band of Brothers win and win and win. In my four years there, I never missed a game... not even a play! I confess... I couldn't because I was in the band. During Coach Bresler's first 1972 season, I was a trumpet player in the Patriot Marching Band (also the first season) and then served as Drum Major for the following three seasons.

And it wasn't just my team, it was my FAMILY! My older brother, Bobby Foreman, #24, was a tailback. What a thrill it was to watch that scrawny, scrappy athlete scamper down the field into the end-zone, adding 6 more points to the scoreboard. In many ways, Bobby represented the fighting character of our then-adolescent team. He was an underdog ball-carrier, not physically impressive, small, sweet, but tough. And so was our team at that time. In general, compared to the greats of that day, like Banks High School, we were considered "underdogs," not impressively big, but like Bobby, good-natured but tough, even mean when provoked; smart and fast on their feet, really fast! Lesson learned... never underestimate the underdog... they have a vicious bite.

My little sister, Margaret was also in the band as a high-stepper, a Star-Spangled Girl. With mom and dad (Bob and Peggy) and brothers (Art and Del Ray), all six of us had a front row seat every Friday night, first at Berry High School field, then the Samford football stadium and then under the bright lights of our newly-minted Waldrop Stadium watching our Bobby and our Patriot Team's March to Victory!

*Background*

As I started this heart-felt attempt to honor this fine man, Alvin Bresler, I was immediately swamped with nostalgic recollections of my life at Homewood High. As one of the first students to rush through the virgin doors of our modernistic academic fortress as a Freshman in December of 1972, I was in awe of its soaring walls, the four brightly-colored pods with matching lockers, doorless classrooms and what seemed more like a college library and auditorium than high school.

The City of Homewood was forty-six years old by then, finally making the break away from the Jefferson County School System, creating its own system, constructing our crowning glory in the muddy basin of what was once a popular Birmingham "get away" in the early 1900's, Edgewood Lake.

Some folks think Homewood has always been, well… Homewood, but that's not the case. Unlike the story of our "new" senior high school and its meteoric three-year ascent to athletic and academic prowess, the City of Homewood took almost thirty years to cobble together.

In 1926 a movement began to merge several of the communities surrounding Birmingham. In September of the same year, Rosedale, Edgewood and Grove Park voted to incorporate under the name "Homewood." The City of Hollywood was annexed into Homewood in 1929. In 1955, Oak Grove was also annexed, completing the Thomas Kinkaid kaleidoscope that we now know and love as Homewood.

Every resident should feel a debt of gratitude to those men and women who gave their lifelong efforts to present to us a fifty-year-old dream, our very own college-prep campus. This stunning, shiny megalith sits across from Samford University on the south bank of Shades Creek, would become the most desired academic high school in the state with superb athletics, band, choir, fine-arts, debate and a plethora of other programs that thrive still.

*A Tribute to the Coach*

It was this storied backdrop that set the stage for twenty-three year-old Alvin Bresler, who was recruited from Anniston High School to Homewood High in 1972. Most of us not on the football team thought of our Head Coach rather iconically. These were the "Bear Bryant / Shug Jordan" days when coaches were giants, revered and even feared. Though very approachable, our young coach carried himself in a way that encouraged respect. After all he was by trade a disciplinarian, and any student including myself, paid homage to him.

Upon arrival in Homewood he set out immediately putting together his team of assistant coaches: Dave Beason, Jackie Clayton, and Wayne Sheets. Bryan Winslow served as our Head Trainer, while the Student Team Manager was Stoney Jackson. Along with others on the large crew providing support, Coach Beason had "deep roots" as he had matriculated through the system from Homewood Junior High, just as I had. We were already a close community when Coach Bresler joined us, an advantage that would propel him to the top of his very competitive career field, at lightning-speed.

Coach Bresler started out a winner, finishing his first season in 1972 with 6 wins and 4 losses. He bettered that in 1973 with a record of 7 and 3. He then finished it off with an amazing record of 13 and 1, culminating with a 10 - 7 victory over Dothan at Legion Field on December 6th ,1974. On that bitterly cold and rainy Friday night, the team was led by quarterback Murray Legg (#12) who had been at the helm for three seasons. With Murray, his Co-Captain, Randy Smith (#62) and his small-town team of tough guys, Coach Alvin Bresler at twenty-six years old engraved his name forever in Alabama High School football lore as the youngest ever to win the coveted Alabama State 4-A Football Championship.

He would be the first to tell you that he could not have accomplished such an amazing feat on his own. He came to our quaint village in-tandem with his beautiful newlywed, Becky. As the old saying goes, "behind every good man is a good woman" and Becky was just that. She provided the loving home and security Alvin needed to kick-off not only his football legacy, but also his family legacy, one that championed three beautiful daughters.

*A Tribute to our Teachers who were also Coaches*

As Drum Major and President of all my classes for three years as well as the SGA, I was fortunate to have regular contact with the bosses, coaches and teachers inside our "halls of higher learning" that deserve highlighting; especially Mr. Michael Gross, our Principal who came with us from our junior high. We dealt together with issues such as "student's rights" when there were threatened "sit-ins" (it was after all the early-mid 70's) and other very sensitive concerns of both students and even faculty.

He was fortunate to have had a very capable Sergeant-at-Arms, Jack Farr, who brought a needed, calming demeanor to our convoluted campus. I had the pleasure to witness their interactions with a few key leaders, including Coach Bresler as they suffered through the legal trials and tribulations of what almost did not become the 1974 Championship Playoffs or the Title. What a discombobulation that was…that's a story that you're going to have to hear straight from Mr. Gross, or the Coach himself. As God would have it, their game plan, both on and off the field proved victorious.

Like all of our teachers at Homewood, who are truly the unsung heroes of my life, Alvin Bresler's coaches/teachers made a huge mark on our school, not only in the making of state champions but in developing boys and girls into men and women, many who went on to become outstanding inter-collegiate athletes, business leaders, service-members, scholars and community servants. I can personally account for a few that had a significant impact on my life.

Coach Clayton served as our Wrestling Coach. My brother, Bobby and I, were on the team in 1974 where we were forced to endure hours of grueling "sit-outs," a move that Coach Clayton had mastered and showed us on numerous occasions. Though Homewood did not have a gymnastics team, he personally encouraged me to continue to develop those talents, which would soon pay off for me as a "walk-on" to the West Point Gymnastics Team.

Coach Mike Miller led an amazing group of musicians and vocalists to continued excellence in choir and fine arts. He was responsible for encouraging one of his choir members, starting defensive tackle and our Class President, Mike Wald (#67) to learn to play the trumpet which he did well- so much so that in only a few months he was featured in uniform (pads and all, right off the field) during our halftime show playing a solo to "Brian's Song," a popular song about Brian Piccolo of the Chicago Bears. Coach Miller could be found on the field, in the choir-room or in the auditorium, if not directing the singing, then building the sets that Patricia Bailey needed for the many plays she directed.

Several of Coach Bresler's players performed in Ms. Bailey's musicals, most notably Reed Rogers (#57), who played the starring role as Conrad Birdie in our 1975 production of "Bye-Bye-Birdie." Many of her students, including myself, achieved the highest honors possible in theater. In May of 1975, Murray Haden and I were declared "State Champions" in our two-man performance of "Gloria Mundi" at the Alabama High School Theater Festival. Like Coach Bresler, Mrs. Bailey brought the science of performing arts, as well as debate to state championship levels.

In addition to being lead coaches for our pigskin Patriots, Coach Beason and Jones were also Head Coaches for our winning varsity basketball team while Coach Sheets coached the varsity baseball team. J. Barncastle coached our Varsity Swim Team. There were several other assistant coaches, such as the happy-go-lucky David Jones, the meticulous Coach Newton and the affable Coach Riley P. (Rip) Harmon from HJHS who were important mentors to us students and especially to the young men who had a talent for tackle football. Along with Stoney as Team Manager, who could forget the inspirational "Class Favorite" Chuck Yow, the always-friendly Bill Gulas, the "Most Dependable" of the Class, David "Crick" Walker along with agreeable Billy Allums. Team Trainer was Palmer Griffin.

Women's athletics were on the move in high schools across the state and Homewood had its fair share of female coach-teachers: Nancy High was the Women's Gymnastics Coach, Barbara Murphy, my tough but fair chemistry teacher, the Tennis Coach, Susan Cook, the Volleyball Coach and Miss Lillie Hawkins was the Archery Coach. *And last but not least Coach Cindy Wade of the Star Spangled Girls was more than a teacher or a coach, she was a mentor for life.*

Coaches, teachers, athletes and students alike toiled together during Homewood High's birthing years, to help make it what it is today... a Community of Champions!

# CHAPTER 1

# A NEW HIGH SCHOOL IN HOMEWOOD, ALABAMA

The first year of Homewood High School consisted of 9th graders and 10th graders who came from the Junior High, 11th graders who were supposed to go to Shades Valley High School but didn't and seniors who had been at Shades Valley as sophomores and juniors. Coming over to the new Homewood High was not easy in some ways, but in others it was a welcome change. At the beginning of the school year, first semester classes were held at the Junior High and at Dawson Memorial Baptist Church just down the road. In January 1973 the new high school opened the doors for the first time.

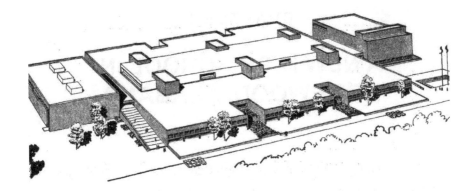

I don't know who designed this school but they were definitely not of traditional ilk. There was a Student Lounge as large as the gym with Patriot themed walls and carpet. There was no furniture so students sat on the floor in groups studying or conversing while they waited for the next bell to ring. There was an Olympic-sized swimming pool, the only one of its kind in Homewood. The auditorium was very large with comfortable seats and all the new high tech components seen in any downtown theater. The locker rooms and coaches' offices were clean and roomy. Each of the four classes had their own classroom areas in what were known as 'pods' which meant they adjoined a big open area near their lockers, so intermingling with other classes was minimal and cut down on bullying. In the center of the school was the library, a first class facility and the heart of the school.

## CHAPTER 2

# FIGHTING PATRIOTS
# FIRST SEASON 1972 -
## NARRATOR BRYAN WINSLOW

Alvin Bresler was twenty-three when he was hired as Head Football Coach at Homewood High School for their first season, 1972, as an over-the-mountain high school. He was twenty-six when they won the 4A State Football Championship, a record to this day. For years after being the youngest coach to ever win the 4A title in Alabama he was asked how he did it? His simple reply, "I had twenty-six seniors, we had no major injuries and the team chemistry was unparalleled in high school in my experience." Coach Bresler was head coach at Homewood in 1972, 1973 and 1974, at Talladega in 1975 and 1976, Vestavia in 1977 with an overall record of 39-25-1. This is the story of how each year built on the last to establish a firm foundation for winning the title.

Most of the boys had played football since they were eight years old and had played together or against each other locally since the sixth grade. By the ninth grade they were all playing together on the same Homewood Junior High team and won 7 and lost 3 games their 9th grade year.

I came to Homewood with Alvin when he had only one year of experience as an Assistant Coach at Anniston High School after his playing days at Auburn. Alvin didn't remember saying it, but he told me after the 1971 season, "Winslow, I want you to come to Birmingham for summer practice if I get this job I'm interviewing for. Bryan, I believe in having a head trainer and your experience in the Army as a medic fits right in with my objectives as a head coach." I showed up without as much as a completed job application from the office of the brand new high school. I became the head trainer for Alvin's first two teams and during the 1974 season I was an EMT watching the games from my ambulance stationed on the track just beyond the east end zone.

Alvin's third team went 13 and 1 and won five of those games by scoring the winning score late in the fourth quarter, two of them with less than two minutes remaining on the clock. As I sat in my ambulance recollecting the two years I served as head trainer, my memory harkened back to that first summer and the two-a-days that started the whole enchilada.

The football team began summer practice in August 1972 by holding two-a-days at Mountain Brook Elementary School, a very nice field and dressing room in Mountain Brook Village. This field was less than a mile from Shades Valley High School and their players would park nearby and watch Homewood's practices, creating the first of many dilemmas for the Homewood seniors. On the one hand, they had played with these Shades Valley boys for two years. On the other they had to go ask them to leave. As Bill Holmes put it, "Going up there to ask them to leave was uncomfortable, to say the least." These dueling emotions provided added pressure for the opening game with the Mounties. Shades Valley had many talented players whom the Homewood seniors knew well, Dana Poe, Marc Merritt, Steve Clark, Marty Jordan... and they knew the coaches extremely well too.

As co-captain Peter Braasch described it, "The change from one type of program to the Alvin Bresler style of football was a breath of fresh air." Dean Snow, one of the starting defensive ends, said, "Shades Valley used a style circa 1950. Once the coaches knew the guys from Homewood wouldn't be coming back to SVHS and they made our lives miserable." Charles Boyd, a starting guard, was more to the point when he said, "Once they knew we wouldn't be back, the head coach took it upon himself to make sure we never forgot and fifty years later, I haven't." For players outside of favor, the SVHS coaches devised a seven on one drill where spearing the lone player in the back when he was on the ground was repeatedly enjoyed by the majority, plus several others who were standing watch. This drill took place under the visitors bleachers, away from any potential prying eyes. Another common practice was after a loss they would decide who was responsible and put them in a brutal tackling drill. One year a young quarterback was singled out and suffered a season ending shoulder injury. "There is no doubt in my mind that if these tactics were in practice today, they would be prosecuted," Boyd added.

The senior boys came to Homewood with these experiences fresh on their minds and to put salt in the wound, it was made known by the SVHS coaches they were supposedly discipline problems and uncoachable. It's fair to say that the new Homewood coaches had a motivated senior class to work with. Braasch went on to say, "The main point, ownership was given to the senior players... an environment where you could be heard."

Many juniors started and played on special teams that first year. They had briefly practiced at Shades Valley one spring training and generally had the same experience as the Homewood seniors had. So there was no lack of motivation for this Homewood team going into the first game of the season. Three Homewood starters that were sophomores, quarterback Murray Legg, linebacker/fullback/jack-of-all-trades, Ricky Powers, and right guard Randy Smith. There were a few other sophomores who got playing time (especially QB David Fleisher) but it was these three starters who made significant contributions to the 1972 Patriots who went 6 and 4 during their first season, with three of those losses coming down to the last few minutes, a record for a first year high school to this day.

We had amazing support from the Homewood High School administration, Principal Michael Gross and Superintendent Virgil Nunn, the City Council and Mayor Bob Waldrop. I had all the tape and medical supplies I needed as Head Trainer and I had two Assistant Trainers to help me provide the boys with top notch physical and medical support. Head Coach Alvin Bresler had the support and budget for first class uniforms, Trailways buses for transportation to games, booster support for pre-game meals and white Patriot polo shirts for game days from local patrons. As Alvin said, "Our goal is to deliver a college-like program for our players and coaches," proving that high school football was changing in the minds of parents, players, coaches, administrators and students because a first class football program can increase the visibility and reputation of an entire city. Bresler didn't know it that first season but putting Homewood on the map and changing the football results of all the over-the-mountain programs was something that he would be credited for as time went on.

The first job Alvin had once he was hired was to assemble a staff. The easy choice was David Beason who had been in the Homewood system for six years and had coached all the boys in Junior High where they had good success and winning seasons in football and basketball. Coach Beason coached the offensive line and worked with Jackie Clayton, who was hired as the Offensive Coordinator. Jackie had been heralded as a great running back at Samford and hired as a coach at Mountain Brook Junior High. He was a well regarded offensive mind which proved to be true over the three years at Homewood. The last position to hire was the Defensive Coordinator, Wayne Sheets, who worked with Alvin on the defense.

Alvin molded a very good secondary in 1972 with Wayne Turnipseed at Safety, Ray Powell Strong Safety, Bill Holmes and Alan Hardin on the corners. Sheets designed the front seven, the stalwart unit of the team, led by Braasch at linebacker and All-State defensive lineman Randy Galbraith. Other standouts were Paul Dougherty, Dean Snow, Charles Mizerany, Ricky Powers, Mike Haltiwanger, Dean Black and Danny

Brechin. Others who saw playing time were Joey Dillon, Rodney Rickels and Randy Dickinson.

The offense was built around the two-way starters Braasch, Hardin, Holmes, Powers and Powell. Murray Legg was developed into a starting quarterback soon after practice began and in an unusual stroke of luck for a high school program, sophomore David Fleisher was an excellent backup quarterback who saw some playing time. The running backs were Chris Moore, Alan Hardin. Peter Braasch, Ricky Powers, Mike Akins, Kenny Turner and Dean Black. Coach Beason worked with an offensive line made up of Charles Boyd and Randy Smith at guard with Charlie Mizerany a reserve, Don Campbell at center, Bryan McFee at right tackle, and Daryl Brown at left tackle; David Barnett was the tight end. Two sophomores, Wade Kirkpatrick and Garry Runyans, were back ups at tight end and tackle respectively and moved in the rotation more as the season went on. The receiving corps was senior Bill Holmes at flanker and junior Ray Powell at split end. Backups with significant playing time included Randy Dickinson and Rick Shamberger. David Barnett was the place kicker and kick off specialist. Senior Rod Nelson was an excellent punter who went on to punt for Alabama.

The final coaching staff hires included Mike Miller, a music teacher and a Student Assistant coach from Samford, Bob Newton and assistant David Jones. They helped Beason with the offensive line. Coach Newton went on to be head football coach at Homewood from 1995 through 2005 and he retired in 2008 having won 5 State Championships, with an overall record of 124-24 and sending many players on to college teams and a couple to the NFL. Coach Jones was the offensive coordinator at Homewood from 1995 to 2010 for 5 of the State Championships. David told me he believes that there are three ingredients to a championship team, "Talent, good coaching and the intangibles, which are chemistry (how the players feel about each other and how they respect the coaches), injuries and depth." These things came together in 1974 and were present in all the championship years since.

The head equipment manager was Rolan Jackson (Stoney), along with the assistants JJ Bischoff, Mike King, Tommy Coleman, Chuck Yow, David Walker, William Gulas and Billy Allums worked very long hours and did an excellent job for their team. Building unity is a part of winning and it includes respect and appreciation shown to all members of the team.

Stoney told me, "It was during my 9th grade year, when I was a manager for basketball, that this man named Alvin Bresler approached me and asked me to be one of the managers for the new Homewood High School football team. I remember from day one that Coach Bresler wanted to establish the best of the best at Homewood. He made everyone on the team, including the managers and trainers feel like they were very important members of the team. He understood that it took a unified team doing our individual jobs to perform at the highest level and accomplish something far beyond our individual capabilities. He was always building on that theme with everything that we did. I remember that he wanted us to look our best so we were fortunate to have first class uniforms. We had first class equipment and we traveled first class. Instead of using the city school buses he would always charter buses so that we traveled in style. He wanted every edge we could get on any team that we played. Until we got our own stadium we played at Berry High School and Samford field. I remember that at Samford there was a walkway that came down the hill in a sideways V and Coach Bresler had the team walk out in single file in our awesome looking uniforms. I think it instilled a quiet confidence in who we were and the mission that we were on."

Regarding team unity, there was another part of Coach Bresler's past and experience that he brought to Homewood. Before the championship season Coach Bresler took the team for a weeklong summer camp in the Cheaha Mountains, just outside Talladega, Alabama. We took our whole team, staff and equipment to Camp Mac and practiced, ate meals and played together for a week. I believe it was one of those things that cemented our unity as a team before we started our championship run that year. Twenty-six seniors, most of whom had grown up together in a small community of Edgewood and the first full four-year graduating class from Homewood High School, had won the 4A State High School Football Championship."

## Chaplain

The team Chaplain was Dr. E.L. McFee, the Head Pastor at Trinity United Methodist Church in Homewood and father of Bryan, our right tackle. I would go to church on Sunday mornings with some of the players who had gone there all of their lives. Dr McFee was a great preacher who always knew how to relate things to what was going on in the lives of his congregants. Alvin said of Dr. McFee, "While living in Anniston we were members of The First United Methodist Church of Anniston. We moved our membership to Trinity United Methodist Church in Homewood at the time that I became the head football coach at Homewood High School in 1972. Dr. McFee was one of the greatest Methodist preachers of 'all time' and I asked him to be our Team Chaplain. He accepted my invitation and made himself available to our football team during the season: (1) For pre-game Vesper Services after our pre-game meals, both home and away games, (2) was present on the sideline for home and away games, (3) was available to players who needed 'off the field' counseling. This became important in summer practice of 1973 when Rick Cunningham's father was killed in a natural gas explosion in Birmingham. Rick and his family were devastated and the team rallied behind them as Dr. McFee delivered a sermon no one could ever forget." By the time the 1974 season began Dr. Charles Gattis became the team Chaplain, he was also a pastor at Trinity, and made the trip to Camp Mac.

As the first season went on I became a part time head trainer and full time player counselor. Many of the boys took to me for several reasons, I think. I was a decorated Vietnam War Veteran who came from Ayer, Massachusetts via Fort McClellan in Anniston, Alabama where I was stationed after my tours of duty were over. Kids were curious about the War with all the protests they had lived through in the late 60's and in the 70's. I was a medic in 'Nam for three tours and earned a Purple Heart for battlefield heroics. This experience provided an air of confidence that transferred to some players just from being around me. Not that I would ever talk about the War even when prodded, but just knowing I had been there with some of their relatives was a comforting air of unity. I was a good listener and capable of straightening out a bad attitude every now and then. As they moved through the games and played established competition, having someone to tell them that "those kids put on their pants one leg at a time just like you do" brought some clarity to the challenge at hand on Friday nights.

The relationships I built with some of them led to a couple of problems with parents and the end of official work there after the 1973 season. Two years as head trainer was rewarding and I would have liked to finish the 1974 season, Alvin's last at Homewood, but it just wasn't in the cards. I maintained many friendships at Homewood with players through their college careers and beyond. It was thanks to Murray Legg that I got an opportunity to be a trainer in 1978 at the University of Alabama where I was Coach Bryant's personal medical assistant, manning the heart defibrillator he had by his side at practice. This was the highlight of my training career and I moved on to become a police officer in Talladega in 1980. My time at Homewood is a cherished time in my life and a special time for all the athletes, students, parents, teachers and all supporters of Homewood Patriot football.

The four losses in the 1972 season were Shades Valley, Tarrant, John Carroll and Erwin but two of them were very close and came down to the last minutes in the 4th quarter to determine the outcome. Coach Bresler knew his team was getting close to meeting its potential in the Homecoming win against Vestavia, other wins were Holt, Midfield, Emma Sansom, Tuscaloosa County and Mountain Brook.

The opening game against Shades Valley started with both teams running the ball and Peter Braasch making a 50 yard run for a touchdown and Randy Dickinson kicking a field goal to take a 10-7 lead at half. Shades Valley found their passing game in the second half with two unanswered TD's to make the final score 20-10.

The second game against Holt at Berry High School field, began with the visitor running back the opening kick 95 yards for the score. Homewood answered with a 68 yard drive with Legg to Powell for the tying score. Holt fumbled a punt and Randy Smith recovered leading to another Homewood touchdown to take a 13-7 lead at half. Holt tied the game on their first possession and Randy Dickinson kicked a field goal in the fourth quarter for a 16-13 first-ever victory for Homewood.

Playing Tarrant at Berry High School field pitted two closely matched teams where the winning score was made by Tarrant, and their star quarterback Jack O'Rear, with twenty-six seconds left in the 4th. Randy Galbraith was the player of the game in a 13-7 loss.

Homewood went to John Carroll stadium for the fourth game of the season. Kenny Turner and Ray Powell had touchdowns and Alan Hardin was the outstanding player in the game for Homewood in a disappointing loss 19-14.

At Midfield, Homewood captured its second win of the season in a 19-0 shut out. Peter Braasch had two scores and Mike Akins a third to secure the win. The defensive effort was outstanding with the Patriot Award going to Randy Galbraith.

A hard fought game at Erwin was another defensive struggle with Erwin scoring the only points of the night in the second quarter. A controversial call in the end zone on the last play of the game where Ray Powell clearly caught the ball in bounds went Erwin's way to preserve their 7-0 win at home.

Homewood's first Homecoming game was played against Vestavia. Homewood scored first on a 60 yard drive capped off with a two yard score by Dean Black. The stingy Homewood defense mounted a goal line stand in the second quarter and Homewood scored again in the third with a David Fleisher quarterback sneak and a Legg to Holmes two point conversion to take a 15 point lead into the fourth. Vestavia scored their lone touchdown late in the fourth and the PAT was missed to end the game with a Homewood homecoming victory 15-6.

Tuscaloosa County began with a 31 yard halfback pass from Alan Hardin to Bill Holmes for the first score. Peter Braasch and Ricky

Powers both had touchdowns in the second half to secure a 21-13 victory for Homewood.

Traveling to Emma Sansom in Gadsden provided for the first Homewood offensive coming out party with Murray Legg passing to Hardin and Powell for first quarter touchdowns and Hardin scoring again on an eight yard run to end the half. Powers and Black had running scores in the second half to provide a 48-12 victory with the outstanding player award going to Legg.

The most memorable game of the 1972 season was the last one against Mountain Brook. These schools had been rivals in elementary and junior high and Mountain Brook had only been a high school for a few years. Homewood's record was 5 and 4 going into this last game and it was going to be a hard fought game against a very good team. Homewood came out on top 6-0.

After the game we were all on the bus when Coach Bresler boarded and addressed the team. In his enthusiastic and commanding manner he coined the new name of the team. "From this win forward we are the Homewood Fighting Patriots," Bresler said, setting the stage for next year's team. Bresler was acknowledging the expectations and standard of winning set by this senior class that had been brought back to their home-town and emerged true winners.

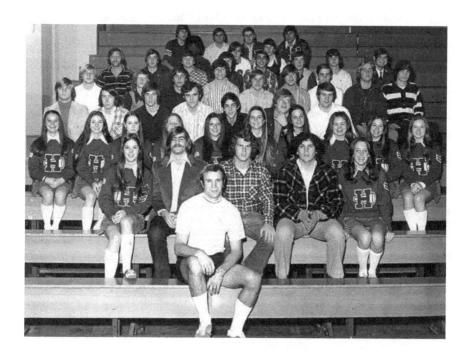

**Susan Steiner Farlow - Head Cheerleader 1972 - My memories of Coach Bresler:**

My Homewood classmates and I were so excited about the prospect of a brand new high school. Even though we were already established as students at Shades Valley HS, we understood that we would be transferring to Homewood HS for our senior year - which meant we would be the FIRST graduating class. Unfortunately, the high school was not completed in September of our senior year so we went to classes at Homewood Junior High and Dawson Memorial Baptist Church. Not exactly ideal, but we were all happy to be a part of this great transition. We were able to help vote on the mascot (Patriots) and our school colors (red/white/blue) and we went about the school year as normal as possible - attending classes, pep rallies, football games, Homecoming parade etc.

I remember hearing about how great Coach Alvin Bresler was even before I met him. He did not disappoint. The guys all loved him because he was a former collegiate player and they had confidence in his knowledge and experience; the girls all loved him because he was young and good looking. I asked and was allowed to work one class period as "coach's assistant" and that was a lot of fun for me. This would never be allowed today, but I remember one of my jobs was to leave school to drop off the football uniforms at the local dry-cleaners. That was pretty cool. Coach Bresler had so much charm and personality and always had a smile on his face. He was a wonderful coach and we had a very successful first year. He was the perfect hire for this up and coming school, always very professional and was a super-great role model for us all. I'm not sure how many years Coach Bresler coached at Homewood, but the impact he made there to all of those who were fortunate enough to know him was immeasurable.

# CHAPTER 3

# 1973 SEASON

Just as 1972 had two standout senior players who led the way for the Fighting Patriots, the 1973 season was stacking up the same. Ray Powell and Alan Hardin were two-way starters as juniors and poised to lead the way as seniors. They both had spent a little bit of time at Shades Valley but like the Homewood boys before them, the coaches didn't have time to work with players they knew were going to be transferring to the new high school across town. There were six or seven from Homewood that did their time at Shades Valley, and according to their recollections all they did was run wind sprints... like Forrest Gump they ran, and they ran, and they ran some more. They didn't stop running until they finally arrived back at Homewood Junior High. A few of these Fighting Patriots who joined Powell and Hardin were Mike Akins, Danny Brechin, Ricky

Kitchens, Rick Shamberger and Randy Dickinson, all of whom were players as seniors who beat Shades Valley very convincingly in 1973.

Ray Powell grew up in the shadows of Shades Valley stadium. As a ten year old he arrived early with his mother who ran the concession stand for the band where Ray's older brother Jim, played the clarinet in the band. Ray and Joe, another Powell boy, spent an hour watching the team warm up from a close view on the track just outside the fence. This 1966 Mounties team starred a wide receiver named Alvin Bresler who was one of the fastest runners in the State of Alabama, even in the entire South. He had soft hands and caught everything within reach of his six three frame. Ray watched Alvin run routes, the details of his moves and acceleration at the right times. He saw how Alvin got separation from defensive backs so the quarterback could get the ball to an open receiver, the go-to guy as he was known. Ray mimicked his mentor, practicing from dawn to dusk as a young boy and along the way he became a star receiver at Homewood, with his hero as his coach. Ray earned All-State honors and signed a football scholarship with Auburn University where he was a starter, just like Bresler.

Alvin Bresler played football and ran track at Shades Valley High School in 1964, 1965 and 1966. His fondest memory of those years was, as he put it, "My head football coach was Coach Bill Legg, who had a strong positive impact on my life as an athlete. Later, I adopted his coaching style and his coaching philosophy. He treated his players with respect and had the ability to communicate with the different player personalities that come with coaching a team sport."

Powell benefited from a rare and exceptional talent at quarterback, the returning starter from 1972, Murray Legg. Legg benefited from a year of pressure packed play under center to return a poised and efficient passer his junior year. Ray Powell was his go-to receiver and they worked hard to become a passing duo seldom found at the high school level. Always compared to the standout QB at Banks High School, Jeff Rutledge, Murray Legg was also a talented runner. "Having Murray at quarterback with a year of experience under his belt and the kind of mobility and outright running back skills he had put us in a unique position to have a very balanced offense in 1973," said Coach Bresler.

In addition to Legg as a runner, the split backfield included starters Alan Hardin and Mike Akins, with Kenny Turner, Dean Black, Bob Foreman and Larry Riffe rounding out the backups who made for an exceptional backfield. Wade Kirkpatrick was the starting tight end along with another junior, Joe Wurtele who complimented Powell as a starting wide receiver. The very talented sophomore Mark Robbins, backed up Powell at split end. Other receivers included Wally Freeman at tight end, Rick Shamberger, Bill Devan, Jerry McCracken, Chuck Rothenstein and Robert VandeLune at wide receiver, all of whom played on Special Teams.

The offensive line had Ricky Kitchens starting at center with Pat Weaver the backup. At guards were Randy Smith and Russell Akins with Tim Calloway the alternate. Randy Dickinson, Jimmy Glass and Garry Runyans were the tackles who moved around based on injuries and opposition. Randy Dickinson was the place kicker and kick off specialist in addition to his roles of tackle on offense and defensive strong safety. Dickinson later received a scholarship to play at the Air Force Academy. David Fleisher and Murray Legg alternated at punter for most of the season.

The 1973 Fighting Patriots were built on strong defense. Just as the year before the front seven and the secondary were experienced, tough, quick and strong competitors. They moved from the 5-2 to the 4-3 with a good deal of agility. Coach Sheets knew his personnel well now in the second year and counted on the reliable, now inside linebacker Rick Powers and a newcomer, standout Tommy Wingo. They were able to move to the ball and stuff the holes effectively. When the defense moved to the 4-3 Randy Smith came in at an outside linebacker position in addition to his starting role at offensive guard. The defensive linemen were returning seniors Danny Brechin, Jimmy Sherk and Dean Black, juniors Richard Andrews, Herman Maxwell, Morris Padgett and Scott Walker. Starting defensive ends were senior Richard Llewellyn and junior Wade Kirkpatrick. The secondary returned Ray Powell at strong safety, Alan Hardin at one corner and Robert VandeLune and Roger Malcolm alternating at the other corner with David Fleisher free safety.

Coach Bresler was there for his players, on and off the field. There were a few players who had off the field issues challenging their ability to play football in 1973. Jimmy Glass says, "In the spring I almost dropped out of school. My family was having problems because of a divorce. I had done all the paperwork to drop out, but Coach Bresler talked to me and helped me through it. I believe if it wasn't for what Coach Bresler and Mr. Gross did for me, my life would have turned out very different. I joined the Navy and became a Firefighter/Paramedic for 31 years."

Wade Kirkpatrick had some discipline problems in school but never anything too serious. During the summer break when his parents went on vacation he had a party at his house. Word spread and there were over one hundred people who showed up with beer and girls from all over the city. The street was lined with beer cans and other trash the next morning when Mr. and Mrs. Kirkpatrick returned home unexpectedly. That was to be the end of Wade's time at Homewood. Mr. Kirkpatrick told him to prepare to enter military school in the fall and he was to inform Coach Bresler he wouldn't be reporting to practice in August. Coach Bresler came to the house a few weeks later and had a serious sit down with Wade and his dad, and Wade was given one more chance to prove he could find the straight and narrow path before it was too late. "If it weren't for Coach Bresler I would have joined the Army in 1973 and missed out on seven more years of football," Kirkpatrick told reporters after they won the 1974 4A Championship.

The most inspirational story of the 1973 team was Alan Hardin. At 5' 9" one hundred and sixty five pounds, he was the hardest hitter on the Fighting Patriots squad from his cornerback position. He had good speed and ran back numerous punts for long gains and touchdowns his senior year, as he had been doing since Little League. After the season, as he prepared to walk-on at Auburn University, Coach Bresler saw him in the corridor and said, "I would wish you luck, but luck has nothing to do with it... it's all about preparation. You see, preparation is the key to success and lack of preparation is preparing for failure." Alan was prepared. He won a scholarship at Auburn after his freshman year and was a three year starter for the War Eagle's at cornerback. Against Florida in Jordan-Hare he came up and tackled a receiver just as he caught the ball. The announcers and media described that hit as the "hit heard round the South." Alan fielded punts for Auburn as well. I got to know Hardin very well, any player that hits that hard at practice and in games on every play is going to be in the training room every day too. There are few players as well regarded as Alan, and he served as a math teacher and coach for twenty-five years in the Hoover school system where he retired in 2012.

Alvin Bresler was a two sport letterman at Auburn and the "other wide receiver" in the Sullivan-Beasley era, along with tight end Dick Smaltz. It was a trio corps of receivers that set many records, of which some hold to this day. Alvin's 85 yard touchdown from Sullivan is 2nd all-time for longest TD from scrimmage and it held first place for 34 years. He was Honorable Mention All-SEC and chosen in the 6th round of the NFL draft in 1971 by the San Francisco 49ers.

Bresler also ran track and as a Freshman and broke the all time AU record in the 120 yard high hurdles and the 440 year intermediate hurdles. Several injuries his sophomore year sidelined him and he had major knee surgery that year. It was this knee injury that ultimately ended his career before he could report to the NFL.

The 1973 team had a record of 7 and 2 when they played Banks in the Crippled Children's Clinic Classic at Legion Field, where they lost 35 to 10. Homewood was giving them all they could handle leading 10 to 7 at the end of the half. The reigning 4A State Champs under the leadership of quarterback Jeff Rutledge came back in the second half, scoring the last touchdown on a long pass after a fake kneel down, with ten seconds left in the game. Running up the score in this manner left a bad taste in Homewood's mouth with a year to think about it before they played again in the 1974 State Playoffs. Homewood being the only team to play both the 3A (John Carroll) and 4A State Champs (Banks), the players and coaches were often asked to compare the two teams. "John Carroll had a great defense. Banks had an amazing offense, so it would have been strength on strength if they had ever played. There is no need for prognostication of this hypothetical game, except to say it would have been a great competition with many future college stars on the field. The number of A's classification would have been a purely moot point," Bresler said to a former sports newscaster friend many years later.

During the summers Coach Bresler helped the players by getting them jobs at places like Bituminous Paving, Pasquale's Pizza and as lifeguards around the city. This is another example of a college-like program at the high school level.

It is important to point out that the attitudes of the coaches, the manner in which they provided constructive criticism to the players at practice and in the games, frequent water and Gatorade breaks without mandatory salt tablets and a trainer to attend to injuries was all a far cry from the old school methods meted out for decades prior. It's not to say that Alvin Bresler was the first or the only coach who had come from a major college program and was determined not to treat players in the way he and others had been treated, but he was probably the first one around the Birmingham area who combined all the "new school" techniques such as the ones mentioned and team movies on Thursday nights, Trailways buses to games, and steak for pre-game meals. This all combined to provide an advantage in team unity and player motivation to win for Alvin and the coaching staff.

One prime example was the film room. Assistant coaches pointed out mistakes and graded the film of each game, going over some player's performances one on one in some situations. But it would be a frequent comment from the rear of the room, "hey so and so, the big eye don't lie," where the head coach would let it be known he's watching and that a player could never escape the view of the camera. Humiliating someone in front of everyone is not what Bresler considered appropriate at the high school level. He got his point across with class and a subtle demeanor.

Other great high school coaches in the Birmingham area at the time included Bob Finley at Berry and Shorty White at Banks. They clearly used techniques more traditional in scope with top flight results. So it's far from an exclusive change in tactics and techniques working with high school players but as Coach Peter Braasch, a Defensive Coordinator at Vestavia High School from 1976 until he retired in 2016 put it, "Alvin's flare for the college-like atmosphere, the added benefits from relating well to players and the resources he brought to bear are reflected in the way many high school programs are run today. These changes began full steam at the turn of the century and Alvin was thirty years ahead of his time for the most part."

The 1973 season began with a resounding victory over Shades Valley 33-0. This was Homewood's closest rival and the win meant a lot to the coaches and players to get a big victory at Samford University stadium.

The Fighting Patriots then beat Holt by two touchdowns and soundly defeated Tarrant 49-12 at Tarrant. They faced John Carroll for the first loss of the season 27-6 in a game that showcased several All State players for John Carroll (Lou Green, Pat LaRock and others) who went on to solid college careers. Homewood rebounded against Walker in a hard fought victory 19-18 and then a resounding win against Vestavia 28-0 for a road victory. Always a tough and close game, Homewood met Erwin at Samford Stadium for what they hoped would be a revenge victory over the Eagles to keep playoff hopes alive, who the Homewood players had never beaten. Homewood went down again 18-15. Homecoming against Tuscaloosa County yielded a 17-0 shut out and then a three touchdown win at home against Emma Sansom. Not qualifying for the playoffs, the Patriots had a choice to make for the final game of the season. They could play the scheduled game at Mountain Brook or play in the Crippled Children's Clinic game against the reigning State Champions, the Banks Jets at Legion Field. The team chose to play Banks and Coach Bresler told the team, "If you want to be the best you have to play the best." After a 10-7 Homewood lead at half, Banks prevailed 35-10 and went on to win the 4A State Championship.

A 7-3 season in the second year was an astounding feat in the eyes of most Homewood fans and other football observers. The players and coaches knew how close they came to a playoff berth but for the loss against Erwin. The 1973 senior class built the next foundational brick for Coach Bresler and the twenty-six returning seniors for 1974.

# CHAPTER 4

# 1974 SEASON, 4A STATE CHAMPIONS

HOMEWOOD'S ALVIN BRESLER, MURRAY LEGG, RANDY ...
Patriot mentor, seated, is Quarterback Club Coach of the Year. (See st...

## "The Fulfilling of a Dream" by Wayne Sheets - Defensive Coordinator

"When does a dream become a reality?" Dreams are only thoughts in the mind, but reality is something we live with every day. Do any of us ever dream of fame and glory, and actually expect to achieve it? When does a person learn to quit dreaming and begin working toward the reality?

The dream started in mid-December, 1973, when a football team began winter work-outs. It took guts for a player to lift weights three days a week and run three miles after he finished. The days in between were filled with eight straight minutes of wrestling eight different people. Then he had three man rolls, running-in-place, agility drills, and quickness drills. He finished by crawling off the mat to throw up. If he couldn't then it was even worse. The next step in the dream came in February when he put on pads in the dead of winter. He had to learn to tackle, block, and try to defeat the man across from him. The team began to wonder if it was worth it.

They wondered if it would not be better to be inside and warm, or out riding with their girlfriends. But they stayed with it because they still had a dream. By the end of spring training the glitter of their dream was beginning to show as a reality. After staying in shape through the summer the players showed up the first of August with the dream still intact. They started slow, working out the kinks. Then came the pads after five days of shorts and learning. The first Saturday scrimmage with the Big Eye in the sky showed all, and the players realized they still had a long way to go to get their dream to reality.

After two weeks of practice at school the whole team: coaches, managers, trainer and chaplain, left for Camp Mac. What does Camp Mac have to do with a dream? Each player learned to polish up the offense and defense, learned to take pride in being the best at what he did. But most of all, they learned to work as a unit, with one goal. They began to love one another, not only on the field but off. Each of them learned to live life the way it was meant to be lived -- with no selfishness or hate. They helped each other with their mistakes and problems. The dream started changing into a reality at Camp Mac.

The first week of school and the first of many steps to reality, Jess Lanier fell in the rain 22-0; Jeff Davis was our first win in the new stadium 21-6; Hueytown was a disappointing loss 30-23; Shades Valley was our second shutout 37-0 and resulted in our being the King of the Valley; Walker was a late 22-18 victory; Minor showed that our offense could do anything 29-24; Vestavia was beaten 21-14; John Carroll was upset minded but failed 27-7; Berry showed our defense had arrived 14-0; Mountain Brook was the combining of offense and defense for the final climb to 48-6. Part of the dream had been fulfilled for the team, as they made the state playoffs, but that meant one more week of extra work and practice. We gained revenge for our loss to Hueytown with a 21-14 victory. Another dream came true with the 12-0 win over Banks. Then the team met the undefeated Anniston Bulldogs and walked away with another victory 18-0. The dream was now only one game from reality. The Game would be against a tough Dothan team. Would the dream be fulfilled or would it fall short as many dreams do?

We began THE Game in a misty rain, the cold was unbearable, and the wind was blowing hard. The team fought to a 3-0 lead, then fell behind 7-3 on a broken-tackle 70-yard run. The half gave everyone time to think of the whole season and what might happen in the final twenty-four minutes of the game. The second half began with a drive that fell short. Defense tightened, and our second drive resulted in a 10-7 score. Then we held on as a last minute pass slid off finger tips of the Dothan receiver to save our 10-7 lead. What had happened? The game was over, the score was still 10-7. What was in our minds? We realized that we no longer had a dream, we were in reality -- State 4A Football Champions of Alabama, 1974.

The team and coaches bowed their heads and gave thanks to the twelfth man who was with them on the field during each play. They thanked

Him for no serious injuries all season, thanked Him for the team unity and love. They thanked Him for they knew that along the way they had help at times when the strength they had alone was not enough. Then everyone who looked up at that scoreboard at Legion Field realized that with hard work, team unity, love of each other and the hand of God, the dream had indeed become a reality."

## Winter Workouts and Spring Training

The 1974 season began in January after the Christmas Holidays at a coaches meeting where they planned the winter workouts, spring training and assessed the ingredients to have what they thought could be a special season. With twenty-six seniors returning, some very talented players on offense and defense and three or four great leaders, it was up to the coaches to devise an overall plan that would maximize this potential.

The winter workouts would include; wrestling, boxing, agility drills, weight training, stop and go sprints, outdoor hill work and would measure the players toughness and willingness to help their teammates get through it, an "All for one and one for all" mindset. By the end of this phase it was clear they had performed to the coach's expectations.

Spring Training allowed the coaches to introduce the Veer offense they had acquired at coaching clinics they attended. All the players were able to begin to learn it except Legg, Edwards and Kirkpatrick who played basketball for Coach Beason. This is just part of having multi-sport athletes in the program. David Fleisher was the first string quarterback executing the Veer and implementing a wide open passing game. Coach Sheets had full attendance from all his defensive unit and they began using the multiple scheme that proved to make it very difficult for opponents to pre- pare. One decision was made that became hard for the returning starters to accept. There would only be two players to start both ways regardless of their performance the previous years, senior and captain Randy Smith at guard and linebacker and junior Mark Robbins at split end and strong safety. Because the coaches were moving so many players around they didn't have to break the news until summer practice began. The strategy had its intended effect on both squads during what became the longest season ever played in Alabama to that point. There was a Spring Jamboree Homewood participated in at Mountain Brook field where all the players got a chance to show what they had learned in off-season and spring practice. The coaches were pleased with the performances they saw and had great optimism for the season ahead.

## Summer Conditioning and Camp Mac

The coaches' plan included a Summer Workout Program intended to have the team 'in shape' when they reported for the hot August pre-season practices. Each position group had a qualifying time they had to make in a mile run at Samford's track. For some, this long distance was difficult regardless of how much they ran to prepare. But according to Coach Bresler, "The vast majority of players made their time. I think the rain that came as they began to run was a godsend for a few of the guys that weren't adept at long distances or a bit overweight." Once the times were recorded for the 40 yard dash the players had three days of practice in shorts and shoulder pads, conditioning, fundamentals drills, installing the offense, defense and special teams before two-a-days and the hitting began.

After a week, the coaches had refined the team to 42 players and their plan called for all of them to play in every game. This was something revolutionary for any era and something the players didn't realize until years later. The plan called for these 42 players to load up on two buses donated by the City of Homewood Recreation Department and head to Camp Mac in the Cheaha Mountains near Talladega for a week of two-a-days practice and bonding that would last a lifetime. It was Coach Bresler's relationship with the McBride family, the owners of the camp where he had worked summers as a counselor, that made this week possible.

Trainers, managers, coaches and the Team Chaplain, Dr. Charles Gaddis a pastor at Trinity made the trip. It was in a team meeting on the very first night when two of the coaches, possibly the least likely got up, and told the players how much they loved them. This is not something that ever happened in football, in Alabama, in the seventies or before, in Homewood, in anyone's experience. But Coach Beason and Coach Clayton did say it to a room full of stunned teenagers; this is where the chemistry began, the unity strengthened and the 1974 Fighting Patriots became a team to reckon with in Alabama high school football that season. Each night included after dinner meetings of offense and defense and a fun time with skits and sing-a-longs to build camaraderie.

Morning practices were in shorts at the camp field and afternoon practices were held at Munford High School ten miles away. Alvin had a close friendship with Coach Grogan who arranged for Homewood to have the high school field to practice on. These afternoon practices were very intense, as anyone who ever went through two-a-days knows all too well. The last night was the last scrimmage and it was a barnburner. The players performed at the highest level the coaches had seen. It was decided that night by the coaches that the goal for the season was the 4A State Championship.

When we returned to Homewood from Camp Mac, we had a few more days of practice before school started, and the change in venue required some finesse and team building by the coaches. Each had his idea of the best way to motivate the players in the wake of two-a-days to get them ready to play the first game in a little more than a week.

While there were no major injuries, Wade Kirkpatrick had not been able to practice until the last scrimmage at Camp Mac due to a foot injury that required he stay off it most of the day. So, when everyone else was up at six to eat and dress for morning practice, Wade would eat and then go back to bed and not wake up until ten when they returned to the cabin.

This had a dual effect: on the positive side he needed to gain some weight and the food at Camp Mac was tremendous. Since he was not practicing and burning calories, he gained a much needed fifteen pounds, making him the biggest offensive lineman at 6'4", 220 pounds. The negative side was just as he was putting some of his temperamental nature behind him so he could be a senior leader, not practicing brought with it some criticism from the other players and concern by the coaches that he might not be ready to play. He had a good scrimmage blocking on the last day of Camp Mac but they could not throw the ball to him because he had injured his hand in a tussle with a teammate in response to the ribbing. Maturity was not occurring as the coaches had wanted to see.

When they returned to Homewood the offensive coaches decided to apply pressure and see if Wade could respond in a positive manner. They awarded him the first ever "loaf award," by giving him a loaf of bread to carry around at team meetings. This had the effect they intended by raising his ire which made him more motivated to work harder and make up for lost time.

On the last practice of preseason in the last drill of the day, Coach Bresler put Powers on defense and Kirkpatrick on offense, one on one with the yardbird, Phillip Pilouris, at running back to see who would win the battle. (In 1975 Phillip rushed for 247 yards against Vestavia including a 96 yard TD, a single game record at the time). On the first play Powers threw Kirkpatrick to the side and made the tackle, bringing cheers from the defense. On the second play Kirkpatrick stood Powers up and drove him out of the hole for the back to score. On the third and last play they stalemated allowing the back to run by, tie goes to the offense. Bresler was happy with what he saw and led the entire team in the last and final cheers of pre-season practice. Wade ate the loaf of bread and kept the much needed weight. It was the third game of the season before Wade got a pass his way, but his blocking had been stellar so they started getting the ball to him, a decision they did not regret.

Having only one major injury in three years is nothing short of a miracle. There were bumps and bruises, shoulders and ankles, but there was only one with major surgery required and that one was to Rick Powers after his sophomore season. He had the knee operation after the season and the only time he missed was winter workout and Spring Training before his junior season. He recovered completely and never reinjured the knee, probably because he was one of the first patients lucky enough to schedule with Dr. Andrews early in his career.

A significant injury involves major surgery and in the mid-seventies knee surgeries were major. Cutting into a knee to repair cartilage or ligaments required weeks of down time and months of rehab with much less of a chance for 100% recovery than there is today with the advances in surgical procedures.

## Offense

The Veer offense is an option running scheme associated with read-option offenses and made famous at the collegiate level by Bill Yeoman's Houston Cougars. It was run primarily on the high school level, with some usage at the collegiate level where the Veer's blocking scheme has been modified as part of the zone blocking system.

The Veer is an effective ball control offense that can help minimize mismatches in a game for a team. However, it can lead to turnovers with pitches and handoff option reads.

(https://en.wikipedia.org/wiki/Veer)

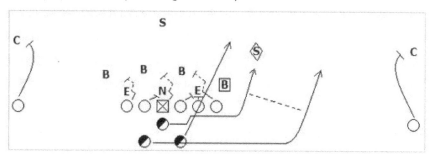

The Homewood coaches attended several coaching clinics in the early summer of 1974, one at The University of Tennessee where they studied and adopted the Veer for the 1974 season. Coach David Jones remembers, "The book we got at the clinic was *The Grass is Greener* by Lou Holtz, was soft bound and only thirty or so pages, but it became our playbook for 1974." There was one overriding reason they were able to make the change, they were 100% certain that they had the type of quarterback that could run the ball properly without mistakes and turnovers common to the risky option aspect of the Veer attack. The offensive coordinator for all three years, Coach Jackie Clayton, implemented the Veer, he and Legg and Edwards worked on the 'pitch' play until they could do it in their sleep. Coach Clayton was instrumental in the strategies that set Homewood apart from the competition on offense. From the passing game to the read-option plays his tough minded spirit resonated in that offense. At Camp Mac when the boys arrived and had been cooped up in the bus for a few hours when they had some free time. Coach Clayton jumped in the pool and took on each player in a dunking contest. With three of the strongest kids on his back he won the battle of the strongest and reminded them who was still King.

In 1972, at one of the Thursday night movies, the boys gathered at the ticket booth to flirt with the young, beautiful lady selling tickets. The boldest of the senior boys introduced her to their single Coach Clayton. He was a bit bashful at first with the players there so they entered the movie. As the film began, Jackie snuck out the door and back to the ticket booth. The rest is history, Jackie married that beautiful lady and they lived happily ever after. These are the stories that matter in our time together at Homewood. Coach Clayton was unavailable for comment for this book but as all the players will tell you he loved his players in football and wrestling and would do anything for them.

A separate blocking scheme was added to the Veer offense that assisted in minimizing the mismatches the offensive line faced in size and strength versus some of their opponents. There was no real name for it so the boys came up with "touch and go" to describe the speed at which they launched from their stance because they could anticipate the snap count based on the quarterback's consistent tone and delivery. There were few offsides penalties and the few times a count on two was called, the quarterback emphasized it in the huddle. Making these mistakes obsolete was a great improvement from the year before. Additionally, the zone blocking scheme allowed for taking the defensive player in the direction they were going, using their momentum to move them because the quarterback and running back were reading these blocks anyway. Overcoming any size disadvantage by the Homewood offensive line made for a great running game not otherwise likely.

Coach Beason was the offensive line coach all three years under Coach Bresler. He was hired at Homewood in 1966 and coached the Junior

High in football, basketball and track. A graduate of Auburn University, David was hired at Homewood out of college and met Mr. Gross, who at that time was a science teacher.

Coach Beason worked with the same three classes in Junior High and at the new high school. Rod Nelson, Peter Braasch, Mike Haltiwanger, Wayne Turnipseed, Ray Powell, Alan Hardin, Randy Dickinson, Rick Powers, Murray Legg, Randy Smith and Wade Kirkpatrick are but a few of the players Coach Beason taught and molded for six years before winning the State and seeing them off to college.

Coach Beason said of Coach Bresler, "Alvin was a great motivator and organized the kind of program he had envisioned from playing at Auburn. He did many things to create a winning atmosphere and positive experience that unified the players and the entire community." In an interview for this book, Beason went on to say, "In 1974 the offensive line was not as big as the first two years, but there was more experience and they had quickness to assist them against bigger and stronger competition. We helped them by devising a method of snap count that allowed them to move off the ball even faster and since we ran the Veer option offense, the combination resulted in a scheme that worked well once we got it implemented,"

Coach Beason was the head basketball coach from the first year the school was opened through the 1982 basketball season, after which he became a school principal in Walker County for the next twenty-five years. He was also a referee for high school football and an umpire for baseball. In Spring of 1996 he was on the baseball field umpiring a game when he experienced a heart attack. They flew him to UAB where he was rushed into the operating room for surgery. As he opened his eyes just before they administered the anesthesia there, seemingly in a dream, was the face of Pat Weaver. Pat smiled at David and said, "Now I've got you right where I want you Coach." Coach Beason said that in that moment a sense of calm came over him and there is no one he would trust more to hold his heart in his hands than Pat. This is the kind of love that was built in the first three years of Homewood football, the kind that lasts a lifetime.

## Defense

Split four to wide tackle six, referred to as a Multiple defense was what Coach Bresler and Coach Sheets put in for 1974. Coach Wayne Sheets was the defensive coordinator all three years and was primarily responsible for the front 7 and Coach Bresler coached the secondary. He put in a Split defense for the first time before the Crippled Children's Clinic game against Banks in 1973. Powers and Smith were the inside linebackers and Wingo played outside in what might be called a rover position. Powers lined up to the tight end (strong) side and Sheets said of Rick, "he was the best athlete we had on defense and had been a starter all three years. Rick was the best linebacker I ever coached in forty years of coaching," he added, "This was also the best linebacking corps I ever coached and the best to play at Homewood." The defensive line was led by juniors Mike Wald and Kevin Scoble with Taylor Wingo at one end and Herman Maxwell at the other. Richard Andrews and Bobby Sherer shared time at tackle and other line positions as needed. Coach Jones remembers the 3'x 5' index cards that Coach Sheets carried in his back pocket, "Wayne would be on the sideline of a game and design the D line scheme on the fly based on what the offense was running and their personnel. He would draw up the alignment for the defense and when they came off the field, he would line them up based on the cards. He was more concerned about the real time factors than he was what the players had practiced all week."

In the secondary, Mark Robbins played Strong Safety and had ten interceptions in 1974, a record that still stands today. "Mark would make an interception in the last two minutes of a game and on the very next play he would catch the winning touchdown pass," Bresler said of Mark.

When asked what he remembered most about coaching with Alvin, Sheets said, "we were preparing to play Anniston who had a great quarterback and two great receivers and he was concerned about playing the same secondary scheme (cover 1) we had played all year. Alvin called down to Auburn and got some advice about a new scheme colleges were running where the cornerbacks came up close to the line (cover 2) and the two safeties played deep to cover half of the field each. This worked well because we held them to 3 yards passing."

Coach Bresler remembers coaching the defense in this way, "We ran a Split 4 as our base defense and could convert into a Wide Tackle 6 on the fly. We would stack our linebackers behind the D tackles to keep them free from blockers to stuff a running attack. Our secondary was somewhat small on the corners but they had better than average speed and were good tacklers. They rarely let an opposing receiver get behind them. The safeties were excellent playmakers."

## Special Teams

The kicking game included field goals and extra points by David Zarzaur in the early part of the season with Tim Calloway taking over kicking duties after the third game as David got more time at running back. Homewood went for two point conversions after many touchdowns and Hank Marshman and Roger Malcolm were on the receiving end of passes from Murray Legg who was the holder. David Fleisher was the punter who did a phenomenal job keeping opponents backed up for the defense. Malcolm came over from John Carroll hoping to see some time at quarterback. He said, "I got here my sophomore year to find Murray Legg and David Fleisher entrenched at the position I coveted. Several of my friends who convinced me to transfer failed to mention that. So I caught two point conversions from them for two years and played defense. Coming to Homewood was still the best move I could have ever made."

Skip Taylor responded to the offer to contribute to this book. Skip was a sophomore running back, backup strong safety and prominent on the special teams. "I remember as a 7th grader the first day of Spring Practice in 1972 like it was yesterday. Being in the lunchroom at the junior high when Alvin addressed the prospective junior high and high school players, challenging us that if we did what he asked we would become state champions some day. I was in awe of him because he had been someone I'd admired and looked up to as long as I could remember. My love for football started at a very early age thanks to my dad who would take me to Shades Valley games as his friend Bill Legg was Shades Valley's head football coach and Alvin was The Mounties star player.

From Shades Valley to Auburn, where my dad was a longtime booster and me still being in grammar school it was pretty darn cool having someone I considered a friend playing on the Auburn football team. Alvin knew me and would pat me on the head and say, "Hey Skipper" and I'd say "Hey Alvin" when we would go to games on the Plains. I'll never forget Alvin making an impossible catch for a TD against a heavily favored Tennessee team at Legion Field and boasting to all those around me, "That's my buddy" and Auburn going on to beat the Vols handily. It was shortly after this game that I received my prized possession, an autographed photo of my buddy Alvin with Pat Sullivan and Terry Beasley. What a combo!

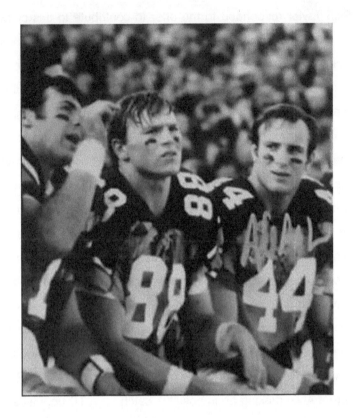

Most of all, I remember later that day after the football meeting at Homewood Junior High he pulled me aside outside the coach's office and told me, "From this day forward you need to call me Coach," and to this day, perhaps because I was the youngest player as a Freshman on the 1973 team, I will forever call him "Coach".

I have so many great memories about those early days of Homewood Football, Camp Mac, a lot of wins, a tough loss, but mostly for me it's the relationships, being the youngest guy I must confess that I really felt pretty darn cool hanging out with the upperclassmen and it was especially good for me since they could drive a car. Having guys like Alan Hardin, Ray Powell, Mike Akins, Jimmy Glass, Wade Kirkpatrick, Murray Legg, David Zarzaur, Jimmy Lee Edwards, Bobby Foreman, Joe Wurtele and Randy

Smith looking out for me was kinda like having a lot of pretty darn cool big brothers.

Our pregame warm-up is to this day "the coolest I've ever seen at any level, and since we only had 42 players, it was well orchestrated". We practiced every week on our entrance onto the field with the precision of a military drill team, Four rows of ten with two captains out front shouting cadence through stretching and calisthenics then concluding with Coach Bresler bringing us together at the end as he barked the final cadence before we broke into groups by position. We probably dressed out half as many as most of our opponents and I recall on many occasions our opponents stopping in awe just to watch us warm up. Moreover, only having 42 players, everyone who made our team had a role and knew he was going to play. Whether on offense, defense or special teams, each player had to be ready to go in at any time. Sure we had a few very talented players, but more importantly everyone played and had a role in the team's success.

Consequently, it made for a highly engaged sideline and fostered a pretty darn cool esprit de corps unparallelled on any team I've ever been associated with. Nothing speaks more loudly to this total team effort than when we were against the ropes, down by 10 late in the 4th quarter that cool, damp evening at Minor High School. If reserve DB Alan Salter hadn't aggressively fought for and recovered our last gasp onside kick with two minutes to play against the Minor Tigers midway through our championship season, we don't get the opportunity to score the go ahead touchdown, we don't win our region, we don't make the playoffs and we're not having this conversation.

As a result of everyone's contribution that championship season, we are forever a Band of Brothers. For that I am eternally grateful and like to say "I credit Coach Bresler" for setting the tone from day one, he cast the vision, he treated us like champions (i.e. chartered buses, pre-game movies just for us at The Alabama Theater and pregame steak dinners), he expected us to prepare, perform and conduct ourselves as champions on and off the field. Even after losing a game early in the 1974 season to Hueytown and trailing late in the game several times, we had a focus, resolve and determination to press through any adversity. Our coaches had pushed us to make certain that we were physically and mentally prepared for any challenge and perhaps most importantly emotionally, we as a team had all bought into the notion that we were destined to be champions.

Thanks Coach Bresler, for not only making us forever champions, but for the valuable life lessons you taught us, for being a mentor to me and many others over the years and most importantly for modeling the importance of aiming high by striving for excellence in every pursuit. Upon reflection I dare say it was all pretty darn cool."

Coach Bresler made the decision to dress out 42 players and play them all based on two factors; he said, "We didn't use but a couple of starters from offense or defense on the special teams and the players had to learn many variations. For example, we had fake punt, fake extra point, several on-side kickoffs, kickoff return plays and punt return plays. We would watch film on the opponent to determine which ones we would implement on Wednesdays before the game. The only area where we had much depth was on the D line so this meant the special team players had important backup roles. While it was done to overcome a weakness it resulted in great team chemistry and a strong will to win."

Rolan Jackson, the Head Equipment Manager all three years said in his remembrance, "This all started years before high school, leading up to our Senior year in 1974-75. There was a group of guys who started elementary school together, and basically played sports together, for a lot of years. Homewood and more specifically, Edgewood was one of those close-knit communities. I remember playing football at Edgewood Elementary with Murray Legg, Joe Wurtele, Wade Kirkpatrick, Pat Weaver, Hank Marshman and others. We played summer baseball together when school was out. Then after sports, we hung out together. We started developing friendships and relationships that little did we know, would really pay off in our high school years. We didn't know what was going on at the time, but in our late elementary years, the City of Homewood started the steps to form its own city school system."

**Unity and Team First**

In 1974, Coach Bresler hired a new Athletic Trainer to replace me (Bryan Winslow), to continue the medical treatment and preventative care for the players. Palmer Griffin, a student at Samford University, joined the team for the first time at Camp Mac. Palmer remembers the time at Homewood fondly and told me he was so pleased to join the Fighting Patriots in the summer of 1974. His recollections include, "Coach Bresler advocated that there be an Athletic Trainer as football is a contact sport that results in injuries to the young men who are participating. A huge part of the journey to the Alabama 4A football championship was the lack of serious injuries so there were few missed practices or games. This is highly unusual for any team but especially important to the fourteen game championship season, the longest game season in Alabama history at the time. The Homewood team held a residential football two-a-days camp at Camp Mac in Munford, Alabama for a week in August of 1974. The week of camp was a great bonding experience for the team and coaches." Palmer met his wife at Camp Mac where they were counselors in 1981 and they currently live and work in Atlanta.

*Palmer Griffin was the head trainer in 1974.*

Coach Bresler had put together the ingredients needed to achieve his goals in 1974: experienced players, team unity, mutual respect, good coaching and support from the entire Homewood community. But as some football guru once said, "It's not the X's and 0's, it's the Jimmy's and the Joe's." We had a Joe, but there was a Jimmy missing. Jimmy Lee Edwards had never played football at Homewood. He had played in elementary school and was a star, but in junior high he was focused on being a very good basketball player which carried over to high school. Legg and Kirkpatrick had played basketball with him and knew him about as well as anyone could. The backfield had lost Hardin, Akins and Turner from the year before, and while the returning backs had a lot of heart and contributed mightily to the 1974 team, something was missing: speed.

No coaches had tried to get Jimmy Lee to come out for football, or maybe they did but to no avail. This was about to change. In early summer Rick Powers got in his 'big blue' Bonneville and drove to Rosedale, where Jimmy Lee lived. He took Wade with him because they had played basketball together. Jimmy Lee got in the car and Rick began to sell, and sell he did. "We need you Scoop. They will build the running game around you. You can return kicks for touchdowns. You will be a star just like at Shades Cahaba." Jimmy Lee looked at Rick and Wade and said, "If I do this thing, play football, there is one thing you have to do, you have to take us home from every practice and every game. If Rick can't do it, Wade has to do it," and he looked at the boys as if that was some herculean ask. "Is that all," Rick asked. "That's all," said Jimmy Lee, and in five simple minutes Rick and Jimmy Lee solved Alvin's "speed" problem, and the Rosedale kids' transportation problem. The rest is history. Every day after practice Jimmy Lee Edwards, Herman Maxwell, and Bobby Shearer (Scoop, Sea Dog and Hamp) would pile in the back of Power's 'big blue' Bonneville and be chauffeured home. Some things are just meant to be.

Some players win trophies. The coaches sing the praises of others and observers have their opinions of the best players on any team. But there are some defined factors that stand the test of time and the scrutiny of writers: first downs, third down conversions, completions and receptions, rushing yards, touchdown passes and catches, turnovers by the offense, three and outs, forced punts, forced fumbles, interceptions, solo tackles, tackles for no gain, sacks, special teams scoring and unforced errors. These statistics show just who was the most responsible for wins and losses and "the big eye don't lie" so there really is a purely objective way of ranking players and squads within a team. No one cares after forty-five years how records are decided. But, as a writer seeking the truth and having to pore through the games, statistics, players and squads in an attempt to tell the best story possible, I can make some unequivocal observations that may explain why we still celebrate this team and have a unique bond all these years later.

The running game (Legg and Edwards) and the linebacking corps (Powers, Smith and Wingo) are, according to stats and coaches, the top two squads in no specific order. The safeties (Robbins and Fleisher) and the receiving corps (Robbins, Wurtele and Kirkpatrick) follow in big and essential plays leading to touchdowns and only one player, Mark Robbins was on both. He was also the only player to make an interception with two minutes left and on the next play catch the winning touchdown. There was only one player who threw for 15 touchdowns and ran for 800 yards, the QB Murray Legg.

The offensive line was inextricably linked to all the aforementioned touchdown plays and the strength and penetration of the defensive line is the reason the linebackers can make plays. The cornerbacks were "bend don't break" and they didn't. Special teams were the 12th Man and the unsung heroes of the year. It took everyone on the team to win games and set any records.

## 1974 Season

The 1974 season opened at Jess Lanier in Bessemer on a muddy field with the rain coming down during most of the game. Homewood won 22-0 on the arm of Murray Legg and the receptions and interceptions by Mark Robbins. Joe Wurtele scored on a 29 yard pass play and Alan Salter, the special teams standout blocked a punt out of the end zone for a 2 point safety. The opener was a resounding win with 118 yards rushing by Riffe, Edwards and Legg behind an experienced line that was certainly opening holes and protecting the passer who threw for 121 yards with no sacks. The shutout was the omen of more things to come from this Homewood defense that had very high expectations coming into the season.

The second game was against Jeff Davis at the brand new Homewood stadium, Waldrop Field, named after Mayor Bob Waldrop who had seen this stadium dream to fruition, along with Virgil Nunn the Superintendent of Homewood schools, Michael Gross the Principal of Homewood High School and the City Council. Jimmy Lee Edwards had his coming out game with two long runs for touchdowns in this 21-6 win against the Montgomery power house. It began as a defensive struggle when in the second period Tommy Wingo recovered a fumble that led to Homewood's 56 yard drive, Legg completed passes to Robbins, and Edwards scampering for the last twenty-four yards around end on the Veer pitch from Legg that would become the go-to run play all year. Blocking was superb by the line. The defense intercepted the Jeff Davis quarter-back Charlie Trotman and the linebacking corps of Powers, Smith and Wingo had a stellar night.

In the second home game in the new stadium Homewood did not fare nearly as well. The Hueytown Gophers handed Homewood its only loss of the season in what was a back and forth, mistake-ridden game with both offense and defense showing they had a long way to go if they were going to meet the goals they had set for themselves. While it was a hard fought game in the rain, the five fumbles, missed blocks and tackles were too much to overcome in the 30-23 defeat. These players had played each other for years dating back to junior high so it was no surprise that the two teams would meet again later in the season. Coach Bresler had a challenge on his hands convincing the team that a loss could be the best thing that could happen to them. Players licked their wounds and put their mistakes behind them for the next game, a trip to the other side of Homewood to Shades Valley.

Always a fierce rival, this Shades Valley team went on to win many games but this night would belong to Homewood. Determined to shake things up, Bresler made some changes for one game. Legg moved to tail back to relieve an injured Jimmy Lee Edwards in the backfield and David Fleisher got the opportunity to get some reps at practice and start at quarterback in the fourth game of the season. They also wanted to get the tight end more involved in the passing game. The changes worked as Fleisher led Homewood to a 37-0 win with a 55 yard touchdown pass to Robbins. Legg had 45 yards rushing and two touchdowns in the first half. He came in on one play at quarterback to run the tight end screen they had been practicing all year and Legg hit Kirkpatrick on the play for a 59 yard touchdown. Legg, Fleisher and Powers all had interceptions to stop Mountie drives. Homecoming was next and things were reset back to normal for another brawl with Walker County.

This hard hitting home game against Walker was not settled until the last 1:11 in the 4th quarter on a diving catch in the end zone by Mark Robbins to culminate a drive where Legg and Edwards shared the running yards. Edwards was back full-speed as he took a Walker kickoff 92 yards for a touchdown. It was a back and forth 22-18 victory with Powers, Smith and Herman Maxwell standing out on defense and with Robbins grabbing the crucial interception and the last second touchdown reception. The media began speculating on Homewood's playoff hopes but there were more good teams to play before that would even be a consideration. The coaches had the Hueytown loss to use to remind the players just how quickly it can all change. Miracles on Friday night were the 'things of champions' and little did they know there was one more coming very soon.

Visiting Minor with their All-State running back, Donnie Robbins, was sure to be a challenge, after all these boys from Dixie Junior High beat the Homewood Junior High kids 44-0 when they were in the 9th Grade. Homewood took the opening possession on a 77 yard scoring drive with a 6 yard TD pass to Wurtele. Minor, with the other Robbins running at will produced two unmatched touchdowns and Homewood found themselves down 14-7 at half. Homewood began the second half the same way with an 84 yard drive with a running TD by Legg to cap it off. Minor drove downfield but the Homewood defense stiffened and held them to a field goal. Trailing now by three Homewood had to punt and the 'Minor' Robbins returned the kick for a TD. Down now by 10 with five minutes to go in the game, the Fighting Patriots drove 55 yards for a score and extra point. Everything was on the line when Calloway executed a beautiful onside kick and Alan Salter recovered it on the Tiger's 47. Legg and Edwards went to work behind the blocking of a determined offensive line and with just over a minute left, on 3rd and ten Legg threw a low pass to the two and Joe Wurtele made the catch of the game 'digging it out' near the ground for a completion. Riffe scored on the next play with a few seconds left on the clock. This miracle win was a complete team effort and the players respect for this Minor team whom these seniors had played since junior high was sincere. Donnie Robbins, the standout running back was headed to Auburn on a football scholarship when he tragically passed away in an auto incident that winter. The tragedy echoed through the halls and locker room at Homewood where the sad news left its mark on long time competitors.

Vestavia was upset minded when they came to Waldrop Field for the seventh game of the season. Coach Bresler knew they were a talented group, well coached and out for revenge from the shutout the year before. Facing another great running back in sophomore Major Ogilvie, the coaches decided it was a week for fundamentals and hitting, especially for the defense that needed work after Minor. He called on the Braasch brothers who were part time coaches to suit up and deliver their hard running blows to the defense. The offense needed to get back to fundamentals as well and Bresler put in a new wrinkle, an end around to the tight end with Russell Akins, the quick and hard hitting pulling guard leading the way. Clayton would have Legg call the play when the time was right. Homewood scored first on a touchdown pass to Mark Robbins with 3:36 left in the first half. Vestavia scored just as the half ended to tie the game at 7. Despite three interceptions by Homewood defenders, Vestavia went up 14 to 7 late in the third quarter. Legg called the tight end around on a second down in their own territory and Kirkpatrick took it thirty yards behind Akins blocking. Running by Edwards and another pass completion to Robbins and one to Wurtele and Homewood was on the nine where Legg took it into the end zone on a bootleg run. Tied now 14-14 with Ogilvie running well, Herman Maxwell capped off a ten tackle night with a sack and on the next play David Fleisher intercepted a pass late in the fourth quarter when Vestavia was threatening. The offense moved the ball the length of the field to score on another Legg run to complete the drive. The upset was thwarted with a 21-14 win.

John Carroll was next and at this point it was clear Homewood had a target on their back with opposing teams eager to ruin the playoff hopes of the Fighting Patriots. This game began in an unusual fashion with Homewood's offense seeming lackadaisical and John Carroll pulling out all the trick plays to tie the score 7-7 at half. Homewood's lone score came on a 65 yard touchdown pass, Legg to Kirkpatrick. It took a Bresler talking to in the locker room to get the team's attention. Homewood got fired up and went on to win 27-7 with two more regular season games to go.

Homewood had not played the powerhouse Berry Bucs before even though they had used their field for home games in 1972. Bresler got them on the schedule as the 8th game of the season and it was sure to be a challenge. The Berry coach, Bob Finley, was a legend in Alabama high school football and they had a defense that was making noise all year. But it was Homewood's defense that "shut out the Berry Bucs, they shut out the Berry Bucs," was the chant, or something like that. The first quarter was scoreless and early in the second quarter Homewood drove 85 yards in 14 plays capping it off with a 25 yard TD pass, Legg to Kirkpatrick to take the 7-0 lead. Tommy Wingo recovered a fumble at the Homewood

35. Legg, Edwards and Kirkpatrick had long runs in a drive that ended in a Legg 11 yard scamper for a TD giving Homewood a 14-0 lead. That would prove to be enough scoring when in the 4th quarter David Vaughn blocked a Berry punt allowing Homewood to run out the clock. One more game to go in the regular season and it seemed nothing could stand in the way of a playoff berth... but nothing can always turn into something before you know it in high school football in Alabama.

Mountain Brook waiting until the last game of the season to have their Homecoming didn't go so well for them. The 49-6 rout was over quickly with Homewood scoring early and often. Touchdowns by Edwards, Legg, Powers on a recovered fumble and Tommy Wingo blocked a punt setting up a Legg to Kirkpatrick score for a 34-0 halftime lead. A Legg-Kirkpatrick pass with a bone crushing block by Wurtele sprung a 60 yard TD run. Legg connected with Robbins on a 22 yard TD for the final score. Homewood completed the regular season with a 9 and 1 record on the same night as the famous Banks-Woodlawn game featuring Jeff Rutledge and Tony Nathan before 50,000 fans at Legion Field.

Now it was time to hurry up and wait. Hurry to anticipate the play-offs but wait to go back to practice. The Alabama High School Athletic Association (AHSAA) ruled a player for the presumed Region 7 champions (Tuscaloosa County) ineligible for being over the age limit. The school hired a number of attorneys and filed a complaint against the AHSAA in their city court. The court ruled the player in question could change his birth date (using a family Bible) thus making the player eligible and the school was allowed to participate in the playoffs. When AHSAA received the court order they had no choice but to rule the player in question eligible and Homewood out of the playoffs.

This ruling rang hollow so the Homewood school administration, along with the city attorney filed an injunction in Jefferson County court to stop the playoffs until a hearing could be held with the AHSAA. Homewood and AHSAA filed a petition with The Alabama State Supreme Court to uphold the decision that this player was ineligible and with the *evidence* presented, the highest court in Alabama ruled in Homewood's favor making them Region 7 champions and allowing the Fighting Patriots into the playoffs. To this day Homewood High School is the only football program to have a case heard before the Alabama State Supreme Court.

The first playoff game was a grudge rematch against Hueytown at their place. Facing the opponent that handed them their only loss, again in the rain, the team and coaches were ready for a fight and that is just what they got. The offense took the opening kickoff and drove the ball 77 yards with Legg scoring from the one yard line. The sure footed Calloway added the PAT for a 7-0 lead. Late in the second quarter Hueytown scored to tie the game 7-7 at half. Hueytown fumbled the opening kickoff and Hank Marshman recovered on the Hueytown 35 yard line. A pass to Wurtele and a run by Legg added another TD and Calloway was true again. The Gophers responded with a tight end reverse for a TD and the game was tied again halfway through the 4th quarter. Homewood took the kickoff and drove down to the twelve yard line and with a 3rd and ten Legg hit Kirkpatrick on a dump pass to the two. First and goal and the Gophers were determined to mount a goal line stand. On 3rd down the Legg-Edwards combo play got the ball over the goalline for the winning score. The defense held Hueytown to a three and out and Homewood ran out the clock, but not until all the Gophers jumped the line and began slugging and kicking out of frustration. The stars of the fight were Taylor Wingo and Roger Malcolm. Homewood headed for the exit with helmets on as rocks peppered the bus. Sportsmanship had left the building.

The remaining playoff games would be held at the famous Legion Field. Alabama and Auburn played there for decades and the Iron Bowl held there every year made Legion Field a favorite TV venue for the entire nation to enjoy each Fall. The 'old gray lady' was beginning to show her age and one thing paint couldn't cover up was the threadbare astroturf which was worn almost to the concrete below. This was dangerous and a subject of debate among college players and fans alike for many years. Coach Bresler talked with experts from the sporting goods business, of which several had supported Homewood with equipment for three years now and they all concluded that Converse tennis shoes would be the best choice for footwear at Legion Field. This was another first and by the Championship Game both teams were wearing them because cleats stuck in the turf and caused injuries.

The second round brought on the Banks Jets at Legion Field in the game Homewood had waited for all year. Shorty White's score with nine seconds left after faking a kneel down in 1973 stuck in the craw of all the coaches and players for over a year. Many thought it was Karma that he lost his star quarterback for the playoffs but the Homewood players didn't care about all that noise, they just wanted to start the game, whoever showed up to play was fine with them. Banks couldn't get the center-QB snap and their first three possessions were fumbles and after the third time Homewood capitalized with a highlight reel off-tackle run by Legg when Runyans and Kirkpatrick caved in the entire right side of the Banks defense leaving a hole big enough to drive a truck through. Legg got the ball to the 3 and one play later David Zarzaur carried the ball into the end zone for 6 points. The PAT was wide right but Calloway would have the chance to make good on the very next possession. Homewood mounted a drive from the 28 to the Banks 12 with a big chunk of yards coming on a great high-wire catch by Wurtele at midfield. Banks stubborn defense held and Calloway kicked a 28 yard field goal making the score 9-0. On the last play of the 3rd quarter Calloway kicked a 29 yard field goal to seal the deal. This was the first time since 1971 that Banks had been shutout and Coach Bresler showed the kind of class he had by not running up the score when clearly he could have.

Chuck Yow, one of Stoney Jackson's trusty sidekicks remembered the story of going to a movie the night before the Banks game. "Just before the 1974 playoff game against Banks, Coach Bresler had this bright idea to take the football team to see a movie. What we didn't know was that we'd be going to see the movie at the theater in Center Point -- right in the heart of Banks Jet country. The movie we saw was "The Longest Yard" which starred Burt Reynolds as a former pro quarterback who'd been sent to prison, and was forced to put a team of inmates together to play against the guards. Well, Reynolds' team was affectionately known as the 'Mean Machine'. After the movie ended and we were all on the bus, some of our players started chanting 'Mean Muh-sheen, Mean Muh-sheen!' and rocking the bus back and forth. That was one of the moments I knew we had a special team that season, and also that Coach Bresler knew exactly what we needed to motivate us to compete with a team like Banks. We were probably the underdog, but you couldn't have told us that night we were going to lose."

The third round, still at Legion Field had Homewood feeling right at home and hosting the undefeated Anniston Bulldogs. The Home team was a decision made in Montgomery by the Alabama High School Athletic Association every week during the playoffs. This round Homewood was to be the Home team and wear their dark jerseys. Anniston showed up wearing their dark jerseys also, in defiance of the ruling. Coach Bresler took it up with the game officials to no avail and in a last minute motivator for his pregame speech, Coach Bresler made it be known that the Anniston team and head coach had little respect for Homewood or the rules we were all to play by. Needless to say it worked.

Led by a top quarterback in the state with two twin speedsters, Anniston was a team different from any Homewood had faced all year. Coach Bresler smelled a possible let down and the sneaking feeling of the killer of any Championship; overconfidence. The coaches poured on the film and game plan preparation to attack this unconventional defense and stop a high octane offense. The Homewood defense was ready and the seniors Powers, the Wingo brothers, VandeLune, Andrews, Fleisher along with junior standouts Robbins, Wald and Scoble were not going to allow a let down, rather they held the twin receivers to only three yards and one catch the entire game. The offense took the ball on the first possession from its own 22 and eight plays later Edwards scampered for a TD. The Legg-Marshman two point conversion had become automatic by this point in the season and Homewood took the 8 point lead into the locker room for half time. The amazing Homewood band entertained the Patriot loyal as they had all year. The offense got it in gear in the second half with a 29 yard field goal by Calloway and a 62 yard bomb from Legg to Robbins. On defense the second half was more of the same with Homewood's defense closing its third shutout in the last five games. Homewood registered its 12th win of the year 18-0 and everyone enjoyed a satisfying Thanksgiving dinner at home with the family.

The 4A State Football Championship was played on Friday, December 6th, 1974 at Legion Field between the Homewood Patriots, a third year school and the Dothan Tigers led by junior phenom quarterback Steadman Shealy and running back Greg Ramsey on offense and linebacker David Dean and giant tackle Gabe Heeter on defense. Homewood, led by senior quarterback Murray Legg on offense and Randy Smith and Rick Powers on defense made for an even matchup on another cold and rainy night in Birmingham. The first quarter exemplified what the night was going to be, a defensive stalemate with only two big plays, one by each team.

Early in the second quarter Homewood drove the ball to the Dothan 19 where fourth down brought on Calloway to boot a 23 yard field goal to take a 3-0 lead. Late in the second quarter Greg Ramsey, the Tiger's running back broke a tackle and out-sprinted the Homewood defense for a 70 yard TD, making the halftime score 7-3 Dothan. In the second half Homewood's offense had several drives that stopped short of scoring and the Homewood defense stiffened and corralled Ramsey for zero rushing yards in the second half. Midway through the 4th quarter Homewood mounted a drive and Legg was able to complete some passes for the first time that night. A mix of Legg and Edwards runs and a Robbins catch for seven and a trusty third down conversion to Kirkpatrick for 13 got them to the Dothan 33.

The patented Legg sweep around right end and a pitch to Edwards just before the defenders clobbered him let Jimmy Lee tightrope the sideline for their big play and the TD that would be the last score of the night. Dothan had one more chance with a Steadman Shealy pass to an open Ramsey in the end zone, as Steadman recalls, "We were so close to winning but the pass slipped off the fingers of Greg Ramsey in the end zone. All I could see was water splashing as the ball hit the turf." It truly is a 'game of inches,' Homewood had two more first downs, and thirty more yards passing than Dothan on the night. But the big difference in the game was Homewood's defense recovering three Dothan fumbles to Homewood's one interception turnover. Murray Legg was the MVP for offense and Dothan's David Dean was the MVP for defense. David has been a Homewood resident since the eighties and his son Beau and Joe Wurtele's son Houston, played together on Homewood's 2004 and 2005 back to back State Championships under Coach Bob Newton. This wrapped up Homewood's 13-1, 1974 State Championship and after the game Coach Alvin Bresler said, "We talked about a state championship at the beginning of the year. It was our ultimate goal; our supreme goal. But little did we know we would be here tonight. We had a great bunch of kids to work with. It's hard to describe how I feel tonight." Legg was a little more pragmatic, saying "I knew we would come back. We had come back all year. Our defense and the offensive line did an outstanding job and our backs ran well. The rain hurt us a little, but we scored enough to win."

## Postseason Observations

The media, experts, and high school fans at large in Alabama attributed the miracle state championship to Cinderella magic that propels certain teams to unlikely championships. I for one have to wonder why? The Fighting Patriots had the best quarterback in the state (15 TD's passing with 800 yards rushing), the best linebacking corps bar none, the best performing group of receivers mentored and developed by one of the best receivers Auburn ever produced, head coach Alvin Bresler. An offensive line with two years of experience under their belt who got off the ball so quickly opposing coaches cried foul to the refs, a running back who was the envy of every coach in the state and four experienced runners to back him up. A 6'4" free safety whose range across the field was unequaled and produced interceptions in the biggest of games at the most opportune time. A strong safety who moved up to the next level at Auburn and earned a tryout in the NFL. A field goal kicker the team could count on like clockwork. Most importantly, twenty-six seniors including five to receive All-State honors, a junior-led defensive line that swarmed to the ball and sacked quarterbacks and plugged the holes as well as any in the state. Reserve leaders who played special teams and filled in for starters without losing a beat. The team had a unity of purpose and a mutual respect for each other taught to them over three years by a coaching staff that expressed their love for them out loud and meant it, something unheard of in high school football.

Cinderella was at a loss for her slipper, the Fighting Patriots wondered why the experts were puzzled. This team was loaded with talent. The backup quarterback would have started for almost every opposing team they played and punted the ball better than any other. The Fighting Patriots won close games, shut out two powerhouses that were never shut out (Berry and Banks), ransacked rivals and did it with class. Call 'em Cinderella if you wish, as they tip their hat to the opponents that fought them tooth and nail to the very end (Jeff Davis, Walker County, Minor, Vestavia, Berry, Hueytown, Banks, Dothan).

One thing that is as clear today as it was forty-five years ago, the twenty-six year old head coach, Alvin Bresler, his staff, and their first three teams set the stage for Homewood kids throughout the following 45 years to believe that they too can win State Championships and they have. As of this writing they have six state championships in 1974, 1995, 2000, 2002, 2004 and 2005 along with seventeen regional championships. In addition, Bresler's blueprint of building a winning program led to other over-the-mountain coaches and teams who had never won a championship to do so in subsequent years.

# CHAPTER 5

# 1974 PLAYERS
## (LISTED IN ORDER OF PLAYING TIME
## OVER THE THREE YEARS)

**Offense**

<u>Murray Legg.</u> The quintessential coach's son. His father Bill Legg was the head football coach at Shades Valley High School from 1956 through 1967. Like Ray Powell, Murray was at the games watching, not just one player, but all of the positions. He was at the practices, the summer camps, hanging out with the players as a six, seven, eight year old. To say this had an impact on his life is an understatement. By the time he got to Homewood Junior High he was not only the best player on the 9th Grade football team, he was the best athlete on the basketball and baseball teams and for the Fighting Patriots he was a coach-on-the-field from the very first year. By the third year he was calling his own plays much of the time. For the other players he was the leader, the go-to person for all things football. He knew everyone's assignments and how to adjust those for specific situations.

There were a few plays in a few games that were the difference makers in the '74 season. In the first playoff game Homewood went to Hueytown to play the team that had beaten them the third game of the season. Hueytown had very good players and the confidence of knowing they had gone to the new Homewood stadium and won by a touchdown. The game went back and forth and the Hueytown defense was tough. Their head coach's son played defensive tackle/end, meaning he lined up differently every play. He was quick as a cat and Brown and Kirkpatrick were not getting him blocked much of the night. Hearn was creating havoc in the backfield and running his mouth at Legg the entire game. It was tied late in the fourth quarter before the Fighting Patriots drove the ball down to the two yard line. It was first and goal and Hearn and his teammates were mounting a goal line stand. It was third and goal and Legg knew what he had to do, he had to run right at Hearn but not leave anything to chance. He told his running back Jimmy Lee Edwards, "See number 90, he's been running his mouth all night. I want you to take him out on this play, Scoop, can you do that?" Jimmy Lee nodded his head and they ran the play to the left. Hearn came across the tackle's face as he had been doing all night heading for Legg with the speed of a badger. Edwards faked the handoff and sent Hearn sailing out of the play, allowing Legg to keep the ball and easily score from the two. This made the difference in continuing to the next playoff game or having an overtime. Or possibly losing a second time and the season being over. Legg had many clutch moments like this as he led his team to win the 4A State Championship.

Bresler said of Legg, "Murray was the son of an outstanding high school head football coach, Coach Bill Legg. Murray had great insight to the game and was a 'coach on the field.' He ran our Veer offense like a college quarterback, which gave us the utmost confidence to give him the free range to change a play that was called from the sideline to what he thought would work. I was extremely proud to see him sign a football scholarship to The University of Alabama."

Legg went on to be a three year starter at strong safety for Alabama and a member of the goal line stand in 1979 when they held on to beat Penn State in the Sugar Bowl and earn a share of the National Championship. Murray was All-SEC and the play caller on the defense. When asked the most important thing he learned from his years in football, he said, "Football is the complete team game. Every player on the team, managers, trainers, all had a role to play. You could not achieve success unless every person involved did their job. Everyone deserves recognition for the part they played."

Randy Smith. A three year starter like Legg and Powers, Randy Smith became an excellent linebacker and the leader on the offensive line at right guard for three years. He was a team Captain in 1974 with Murray Legg and provided strong leadership on and off the field.

One of Randy's favorite stories is against Berry when their best defensive player, the middle linebacker, kicked Smith in the mouth prior to the first play from scrimmage. The player was ejected from the game and when asked what he said to make the linebacker so angry, Smith said, "I don't know for sure but it may have had something to do with his mother." Randy was the jokester of the offensive line.

Randy Smith became a police officer after high school and served valiantly. He was shot in the head by friendly fire in a domestic violence call in 1995. Randy survived and underwent over forty surgeries during the next twenty years. In 2008 his teammates raised $40,000 at a community benefit and created the Randy Smith Scholarship at Homewood High School that was awarded for ten years to the athlete who demonstrated bravery in the face of high challenges. If possible, proceeds from this book are going to be used to renew this scholarship fund. The alternative will be donations to a children's charity. Randy lives in Hoover, AL.

Wade Kirkpatrick. An average player throughout most of his career, he blossomed as a senior and became one of three equal weapons on the heralded Homewood receiving corps. "Wade was a good blocker from his tight end position and had good hands. He caught passes over the middle and downfield and ran well with the ball after the catch. Wade became a go-to target and we had several plays designed to get him the ball quickly so he could run with it. Wade was one of our key senior leaders and one of our best athletes. At 6'4" he was one of the top tight end prospects in 1974, who was an outstanding blocking tight end and could catch and run the football like a wide receiver. I was very proud to see him sign a college scholarship to LSU," Coach Bresler said.

Wade signed a football scholarship to LSU and spent two years on the scout team. He transferred to UNA in 1978 and was a two year letterman. Wade worked in the PC software business for thirty years and wrote his first novel, *Lightning Storm,* published in 2019. He writes under the pen name Patrick Kirk. Wade lives in south Shelby County.

Joe Wurtele. Joe was Legg's favorite receiver from sixth grade through their senior year. He had hands that seemed like they had suction cups for the ball. When asked about Joe, Legg always related the last second catch on the two yard line in the Minor game where Joe had to drop to his knees and "dig one out" like a shortstop. That was one of those few plays that without the catch Homewood would not have made the playoffs. Legg often said of Joe, "He had the best hands I ever saw, until I saw Ozzie Newsome play."

Joe has lived in Homewood all his life and his oldest son Houston played wide receiver on the 2002 Homewood State Championship team under Coach Bob Newton.

**Yes, he caught that.**

Russell Akins. A two year starter at left guard, Russell was the smallest of the offensive linemen but was also the quickest and hit every bit as hard as anyone else. As a pulling guard Russell was able to get out front and take on either an end or a cornerback, a rare agility and blocking ability.

Russ became a corporate Executive in Atlanta at a young age.

Garry Runyans. A three year letterman and two year starter at right tackle, Garry took on defensive tackles that outweighed him by thirty or more pounds. As an accomplished wrestler he was able to maneuver this into an advantage. Garry took on Gabe Heeter in the Dothan game and had the block that sprung the touchdown run by Edwards.

It is CIV USARMY CEHNC, Garry Runyans, a retired civilian Army engineer who has served his nation for over 35 years.

Pat Weaver. Pat was a backup center his junior year and an All-State player his senior year. He was voted Most Valuable Lineman by the coaches and players at the end of the 1974 season. Like Wurtele and Kirkpatrick, he had played with Legg since Edgewood elementary and was his center in 6th, 9th and 12th grades.

Pat served at UAB as a RN for 35 years and is a highly sought after surgical nurse today.

Jimmy Lee Edwards. Fast, elusive and strong as an ox, Jimmy Lee, Scoop as he was known to his friends, provided a great complement to Legg as they ran the Veer offense with great success. It was a common practice for Jimmy Lee to take the ball around end as Legg pitched it at the last second, and run it down the sideline for a touchdown. He ran several punts all the way back to the end zone as well, killing the will of Homewood opponents. Jimmy Lee is retired and living in Birmingham.

David Zarzaur. Part of the deep reserve of running backs, David transferred to Homewood his senior year, was the tallest of the backs and had the ability to slide in and out of traffic up the middle and off tackle. David is the artist of the bunch, crafting the most beautiful ceramic footballs and other memorabilia to Alabama and Auburn football fans. David is retired and living in Birmingham.

Bill Brown. The starting left tackle as a junior, Bill was the biggest of the interior lineman giving the team a bit of size and agility. Bill had the most gregarious personality on the 1974 team and kept his teammates laughing when things became challenging. Bill served in the Navy and is retired and lives in Vestavia.

Larry Riffe. A running back with hardnose hitting ability. Larry did a great job of blocking for Jimmy Lee. He also knew how to run north and south and got the majority of carries up the middle. Larry died in 2016 after thirty years as a cable and telecom lineman.

Bob Foreman. One of several scatbacks and a two-year letterman, Bob was a quick and elusive runner. Before contact lenses were practical on the football field Bob wore thick, black-rim glasses as his radar to find open holes in the line. Bob, his wife Nancy and many of his seven children have owned and operated a jewelry store in Homewood for over forty years, providing a place for old teammates to meet and keep in touch.

Ben Lord. A junior backup to Randy Smith, Ben began starting and playing more as the season went on because of his improvement and to give Smith a breather from his role of playing offense and defense.

Ben is a corporate executive in Birmingham.

Chris McIntosh. Chris was Akins' backup at guard. Only a sophomore, he played more as the season went on. In the playoffs he was on a consistent rotation with Akins. Chris lives in Biloxi, MS.

Tim Calloway. An excellent kick off and field goal kicker, Tim provided a steady confidence to the three point plays Homewood depended on for many victories. He kicked two field goals against Banks and the three point difference in the victory over Dothan in the Championship Game. Tim owns an insurance company in Birmingham.

**Defense**

Rick Powers. The son of a Woodlawn football player, Rick was a middle linebacker in the truest sense of the word. A nose for the football, the speed to get there before anyone else and the strength to deliver a hit on a running back that was the envy of Homewood players and the opposition as well. "With Legg on offense and Powers on defense we knew we could win any game we played," said Wade Kirkpatrick, someone who had played football with both of these guys since they were in the third grade.

Powers entered the 1972 season after a spring practice that proved he was good enough to be a starter as a sophomore. One of the hardest hitters, quickest to the ball and able to play multiple positions on defense and offense, it was his football intellect that people underestimated.

Powers signed a football scholarship to Tennessee and played on special teams as a freshman. He was 2nd team and saw considerable playing time at outside linebacker as a sophomore before an off-the-field incident in a dorm parking lot tragically ended his career the summer before his junior year. Rick loved the game of football and this incident forever changed him. He lived in Birmingham and worked in industrial sales until his untimely death in 2005. Coach Bresler said of Rick, "Rick was a natural born linebacker and possessed all of the qualities of a major college linebacker. He had the speed (4.55 - 40 yd dash), toughness and the ability to destroy running backs. I was proud to see him sign a football scholarship to The University of Tennessee."

David Fleisher. Another player who was a three year contributor for Bresler, David was a quarterback that would have been a starting quarterback almost anywhere else. Legg was only injured once, in his sophomore year, and missed one game. But having David in reserve gave the coaches great relief. As a starter at Free Safety for two years David's range at 6'4" and the ability to make interceptions just at the needed time made him the lynchpin of the secondary. Bresler said, "David was a silent leader and had great respect from the team and coaches. He was our starting safety for two years and like Murray, was a 'coach' on the defensive side of the ball. He had a great ability to find the ball and make a play."

David was the President of the Student Body his senior year and an outstanding student at Homewood and at the University of Alabama. He received a degree in Accounting and excelled as a CFO in his career. David fought brain cancer and beat it three times until 2015 at age 58, when he passed from the return of the disease.

Tommy Wingo. A two year starter, Tommy rounded out the stout lineback-ing corps with Powers and Smith. Tommy's quickness and toughness made him a complementary player on the Homewood defense.

Transferring to Homewood from Ramsay his sophomore year he was immediately named a starter for the 1973 season. Tommy's brother Taylor, transferred for the 1974 school year and their transfers became the focus of an investigation by Bubba Scott, the State of Alabama Athletic Director, when a former Ramsay coach raised the question of whether they actually moved to Homewood. Mr. Scott found that they did after a contentious visit to their house in Homewood. This visit cleared up any questions and helped the City of Homewood *prevail in a lawsuit* that deter-mined which team was to represent Region 7 in the state playoffs. Tommy lives in Homewood and works in sales.

Mark Robbins. A hard working achiever, Mark became a two-way starter his junior year in 1974. He was the best performing receiver and a regular target for long touchdown passes from Legg. It was on defense where he surprised his coaches with 10 interceptions for the season. Bresler said, "Mark was a junior on the 1974 team, but played like a senior. He was the only player that started both ways all year; a wide receiver on offense and strong safety on defense and a true playmaker at both positions. I was extremely happy to see him sign a football scholarship to my alma mater, Auburn University in 1975."

Mark signed a football scholarship to Auburn and was a three year letterman, starting games his junior and senior seasons. He signed a free agent contract with the Buffalo Bills and was cut prior to the regular season. Mark returned to Auburn to complete his BS degree in Business Administration and has had a 35 year career with AT&T.

Mark's fondest memories of being a Fighting Patriot are: "The bond that was created with my fellow teammates and coaches that has continued for forty plus years. The vespers services before games and the spiritual growth shared during those meetings. The bus rides to games with police escorts. The off-season workouts where we had to challenge each other in the weight room and mat room. Winning games when no one else thought we would. Our pregame warmups – seeing our opponents watch us when we went through our line-up and routine."

Mike Wald. A junior standout and starting defensive tackle, Mike was the leader of a deep and talented defensive line. Mike was the strongest player on the team and Coach Bresler said, "Mike played hard on every play and had the talent to break the will of opposing blockers. Our junior D line was the most surprising element of 1974 and made it possible for the linebacking corps to achieve what they did."

Mike is a real estate expert and has sold houses over the mountain for more than thirty years.

Herman Maxwell. A two year letterman, the senior defensive end started and alternated with other pass rushers to provide a depth on the defense. Herman played football and ran track in high school and college and received a football scholarship to The University of Louisville. Herman became a pastor in Birmingham where he has a large and faithful congregation.

Morris "Junior" Padgett. Junior was the heartbeat of the team. He led the cheering at the end of every practice and before every game. As a backup defensive tackle he was in the rotation Coach Sheets had in place. Coach Bresler said of Junior, "The key leader of our team and on our special teams, Junior kept the morale at a high level throughout the year. He led the team roundup after the Wednesday practice and most importantly the 'JP Dance' that we all participated in."

Junior followed in his father's footsteps to become a successful businessman and entrepreneur. Junior lives in Clanton, AL.

Kevin Scoble. A fireplug of a defensive tackle, Kevin hit as hard as anyone on the team. He and Wald provided a stalwart starting line that plugged up holes and rushed the passer. Kevin lives in Murfreesboro, TN and has a career as an airline pilot.

Bobby Shearer. Another defensive tackle in the rotation, Bobby came from obscurity to play on the 1974 team and be recognized as the Most Improved Player by the coaches and players. Bobby lives in Homewood.

Richard Andrews. A two year contributor to the defense, Richard came into his own at the end of the 1974 season and was 'all over the field' making tackles and rushing the quarterback in the playoffs. Richard was an accomplished technician at UAB for over 25 years, where he retired in 2019. Richard lives in Birmingham.

Taylor Wingo. A senior starting defensive end, Taylor "held contain" as well as anyone and was in on the tackle as he provided pursuit from the back-side. He was another great pass rusher and provided a spark with his hard hitting style. Taylor is a construction expert and lives in Vestavia.

Robert VandeLune. A two year starter at cornerback, Robert was responsible for breaking up passes and coming up on run support. As the smallest player on the defense, Robert was hard hitting, quick and never let receivers get behind him. Robert is a retired executive in the healthcare industry and lives in Dothan.

Hank Marshman. A junior starting cornerback, Hank provided the same strength on the opposite side from Robert. Hank was on the extra point squad and connected with Legg on many two-point conversions throughout the 1974 season. Hank lives in North Carolina and leads a ministry.

Roger Malcolm. A flexible backup in the secondary and special teams standout for two years, Roger was the 'enforcer' providing the hard hitting style Homewood was known for. Roger attended UAB and is a biomedical engineer. He runs and owns a medical components company in Orange County, CA that he founded in 1985. As of this writing Roger owns or co-owns twenty U.S. Patents. No photo available, for reasons of national security!

Alan Salter. A senior special teams standout, Alan was responsible for recovering Calloway's brilliant onside kick at the end of the Minor game, giving the offense the opportunity to complete the comeback game of the year. Without this recovery Homewood would not have made the playoffs.

Homewood players, coaches and fans recognize this as the most important single play in Coach Bresler's three year run. Alan lives in Hoover, AL.

Rick Cunningham, Courtney Crowder, Reed Rogers, David Williams, David Dozier, David Vaughn, Joey Gagliano, Philip Pillouris, Wayne Buckley, Stuart Propst, Skip Taylor, Maury Wald and Jerry Winstead all provided crucial back-up and special teams roles and it is important to point out that everyone who dressed out got to play at some point in every game. These players were known as the 12th man and were as important to the team as any of the starters. Coach Bresler knew how to keep unity by allowing everyone to have a role and see some playing time. This was another attribute seldom seen in high school football in the 70's.

## Tribute to a Winner

**Randall V. "Randy" Smith** is a former Birmingham police officer severely injured in a friendly fire incident in 1995. Smith grew up in Homewood, where he co-captained the Homewood High School football team that won the state championship in 1974. Smith went on to join the Army before becoming a Birmingham police officer.

On March 22, 1995, Smith and other officers were called to a 3:00 AM domestic dispute in Ensley. Upon arrival, officers were told an armed man who had already fired two shots was inside along with a toddler. Smith entered the house, retrieved the toddler, and went out the back door, where he was accidentally shot in the right cheek by a fellow officer. The bullet caused brain damage. The officer was later demoted because of the incident, being charged with several violations of department rules.

Smith spent weeks in a coma after undergoing hours of surgery at University Hospital. He was later transferred to Spain Rehabilitation Center. After months of rehab, he returned home to Pleasant Grove on October 4, 1995. Smith's injuries resulted in deafness in one ear, blindness in one eye, and slowness in speech. He has endured multiple surgeries, including plastic surgery.

Smith still receives workers compensation, but his teammates and friends have done fundraisers to help pay for some expenses. He also visits patients at the Lakeshore Foundation and Alabama Head Injury Foundation to share his experiences. He was appointed grand marshal of the 2008 We Love Homewood Day parade and received a Quality of Life award from the mayor. Smith's teammates also organized the Randy Smith Scholarship awarded to a Homewood High School senior athlete who exemplifies spirit and determination *(https://www.bhamwiki.com/w/ Randy_Smith)*.

This wiki, found online covers the facts, but this tribute needs to tell the rest of the story. Randy's bravery in the face of over forty surgeries over twenty years and his ability to remain positive and keep his amazing sense of humor is a true testament to who he was on the first three Fighting Patriot teams.

It is impossible to adequately describe the character, integrity and bravery it takes to persevere in his situation. Toughness was always a strong point for Randy and it certainly came through in his life as a hero. The small child he rescued from that dangerous house has voiced his appreciation, which few people can truly understand. As for the officer who mistakenly shot Randy, he had to live with that crucial error which is punishment enough, and Randy never spoke ill of the guy.

In 2007, when we came together as a team again to form a Foundation, we raised forty thousand dollars at an event in Homewood and created the Randy Smith Scholarship at Homewood High School. The scholarship fund granted $1500 to the senior athlete who overcame the most obstacles in their given sport. This scholarship was awarded for ten years. We gave the remainder to a charity in Georgia that takes care of families of police officers killed in the line of duty. Randy attended every one of the award days and introduced himself to the recipient and wished them luck.

Coach Bresler said of Randy, "Of all our players that gave us (the coaches) 110% in practice and in games, Randy Smith would be number one. His "Will" to want to be the best that he could be exemplified his high school football career and his adult life. His toughness and 'Never Give Up Attitude,' as a football player followed him in his career in law enforcement as did his 'Will To Live!' "

We have had players from those teams to go on to extremely successful careers and more than a few are regarded as high achievers. There are none who achieved the height Randy did in one shining moment when he gave it all for another human, sacrificing himself at the same time. I would say that this is a universally agreed upon accolade by all the members of the Fighting Patriots.

# CHAPTER 6

# THE COACH

Records are meant to be broken but some have not been in 45 years:

Youngest school in Alabama to have a winning record

Youngest school to win a 4A State Championship

Youngest Coach to to win a 4A State Championship

Youngest coaching staff to do all of the above

First over-the-mountain school to win a 4A State Championship

Player with most interceptions (10) in a single Homewood season.

Only Homewood player to start on a D1 college National Championship team

Only team to play all 42 players in every game of the season.

Most games played in a single season.

Coach Bresler produced a dozen players who earned college scholarships and walk-ons that became starters and lettermen. He did this in three years. College bound players:

Randy Galbraith - All State to Auburn

Rod Nelson - to Alabama

Bryan McFee - to Wyoming

Ray Powell - All State starter at Auburn

Alan Hardin - three year starter at Auburn

Randy Dickinson - to Air Force Academy

Murray Legg - All State, All SEC, three year starter at Alabama

Rick Powers - All State to Tennessee

Wade Kirkpatrick - All State to LSU/ UNA

Herman Maxwell - to University of Louisville for football and track

Mark Robbins - All State starter at Auburn

Jerry Winstead - to Clemson.

-- note. Randy Smith, David Fleisher and Jimmy Lee Edwards could have played at the next level but chose not to.

### Alvin Bresler - Business Career

After coaching, Bresler started a career in the surety bond and contractor's insurance industry. Bresler began working with Engel-House/ Corroon & Black in 1978, which is now Willis Tower and he interviewed with the legendary surety bond producer, Frank "Pig" House. Bresler said, "He told me he would make me successful in the construction industry in the surety bond/contractor insurance arena. He said that contractors are like football coaches - they are self-confident, they work hard and they are loyal, humble people. That was enough for me."

In April 1999, Bresler moved to J. Smith Lanier & Co. to start a Birmingham office with four employees, became co-managing director March of 2000, and supervised 42 employees. During the course of his career, Bresler earned the trust of those he encountered and always brought a level of dedication, determination and professionalism to the job every day. His customers and clients all knew they were working with a professional when they worked with Bresler.

During his career, Alvin began attending many Alabama AGC events while serving on different committees, including extensive involvement with the state convention committee. He served as the AGC State Associate Board president in 1998 and in 2003 was the recipient of the Henry T. Hagood, Jr. Associate Leadership Award. Bresler retired from J. Smith Lanier in December of 2019 after twenty years of service.

Coach Bresler and his wife Becky will celebrate their 50th wedding anniversary on June 13, 2020. They have three daughters and three sons-in-laws Robert & Tracy Stephens, Matt & Kelly Rainer and Bo & Jenny Evans, as well as 10 grandchildren.

# CHAPTER 7

# COMMUNITY

*"Winning is a coordinated effort of the team, the coaches, the students, faculty and administration and the entire community."*
-- Coach Alvin Bresler

Even at the young age of twenty-three, Alvin knew the importance of community, inclusion and making it his job to know everyone he could in Homewood and make sure they were on board with supporting the football program. Being a 'people person' came naturally to him.

The students were involved in the pep rallies and cheering in the stands at the games. The cheerleaders, band, majorettes and Star-Spangled Girls put on an amazing show at halftime and became the preeminent program in the state of Alabama, and is today. The parents, boosters club, Administration, City Officials and Mayor Bob Waldrop were helpful in every way and front and center at the Home games all three years. Police escorts to all the games and home afterwards showed how much priority was placed on safety.

## Cheerleaders - 1974

*Melinda McDaniel Leavelle.* I really can't think of anything more fun than high school football in the 1970's! I think it was a special time for lots of folks, judging from the popularity of movies like 'Radio', 'Woodlawn', and 'Remember the Titans.' Those movies bring back so many wonderful memories for me. In a small town like Homewood, football brought the entire community together. On Thursday nights, everybody was at the high school stadium to support the Homewood Junior High Indians and on Fridays, everybody was there to watch high school ball. Originally, we cheered for the Shades Valley Mounties, but by the time I was in the 9th grade, the Homewood Patriots were born. It was a marvelous experience to be able to cheer in that atmosphere.

As I've grown older, I realized just what a unique situation we had those first three years of Homewood High School. Mr. Gross was our own "Mal Moore" and Alvin Bresler was Homewood's "Nick Saban" for all intents and purposes. What Coach Bresler was able to do with our players in three years was just remarkable, although I didn't realize how incredible it was until many years later. I once had a conversation with an assistant coach here in Tuscaloosa and mentioned how many of our players earned scholarships at the college level and won the state championship in the third year of existence. He was very impressed and remarked that he had never heard of such an unusual circumstance for a high school coach and team. It hit home with me then that Coach Bresler had performed some kind of football miracle in his short time at Homewood. Obviously we had an amazing group of boys in our little town, but Coach Bresler and his staff had the keys to unlock their talents.

I know all my friends who played football were crazy about Coach Bresler, but so were the cheerleaders. He was very kind to us even though I'm sure we got on his nerves. He never failed to greet us in the hallways, never turned down a request of ours to do something for the players, always encouraged player participation at the pep rallies, and made us feel included as part of the team. It makes me sad that my own children did not have that kind of high school experience, but I am grateful that I did. It was a time that I have always cherished.

## The Star Spangled Girls - Loretta Burton Strouss - 1972

Posters appeared in the halls all over the junior high announcing Cheerleader tryouts. As a shy 8th grader I thought it would be fun to see what it was like to try out. Momma said yes and I went. I was terrible, couldn't yell or jump but it was fun trying. I obviously failed and was sent packing. About two weeks later posters covered the halls with the opportunity to try out for the new dance line. Well, here we go again. I asked Momma if I could go. She thought it was a sure thing I would not make the line because I had no dance training. She let me go, confident that nothing would come of the experience.

It was incredible! Older girls taught us routines, we danced with pom pom's and learned kick routines. The week flew by and it was time for try-outs. No one was more surprised than me and my Momma when I made the dance line. We met in a classroom to hear Mrs. Wade explain what we would be doing, our summer schedule and then the opportunity to name the dance line. Many names were suggested and considered but it came down to 'Starletts' or 'Star Spangled Girls'. We were born that day in 1972.

Because we were children we needed leadership and guidance. Mrs. Cindy Wade was hired by Mr. Gross and she came to Homewood from being the Director of the Shades Valley Mountiettes. This was not Mrs. Wade's first rodeo and very soon we saw she was strength, determination and cajun spice with a side of Italian meatballs all rolled up into a diminutive fireball straight from the French Quarter. She ruled with an iron will and a battery powered boombox. She smiled, sweet talked, cursed and clawed her way through policemen, coaches, principals and band directors to make sure we were seen and protected wherever we went. She fought for our place on the field and in the school. No one did it better.

Our first practice was in a field next to the junior high on the first Monday after the 4th of July in 1972. We danced in the tall grass up to our knees in the July sun with only a water fountain to keep us going. No shade, no bathrooms, no nothing and we loved it. Four weeks later Mrs. Wade had turned this ragtag gaggle of ponytailed girls into a precision dance team all moving in unison to those blaring beats from the beleaguered boombox. We went off to a week of dance camp at Samford

University and returned to learn the field show with the rest of the band in Dawson Memorial Church parking lot.

Before we knew it the first football game was upon us. The musicians, color guard, rifles and majorettes performed right beside us. We had become a band, small but mighty and filled with a patriotic spirit that was unbounded. Being a member of the band allowed us to attend every game, home and away. We traveled on two Birmingham transit buses praying all the way, hoping the buses would make it up the hills. Sometimes we had to double up but we always made it to the games.

It was magic when we all came together, unaware of the impact we would have on future students. We simply gave our best efforts and enjoyed the opportunity to start school traditions and build a reputation of excellence.

Home games were played at Berry High School field the first year and at Samford University Field the second. In 1974 the Homewood stadium named for Mayor Waldrop opened in time for the football season. We cheered and screamed for our Fighting Patriots with a renewed enthusiasm because we were becoming a school that could really play football. It was so exciting to attend the new school and now we placed the candles on the cake with that beautiful new stadium. We must have started something special because soon, very soon, great things would happen for Homewood High School.

After a full regular season we made the 4A state playoffs and the incredible team would take us all the way to the state championship. We played and danced our hearts out at Legion Field. With hard work and great skill our team reached the highest honor possible and it all seemed like an impossible dream. Coach Alvin Bresler had become the youngest coach to ever reach the state championship in Alabama. He did not do it alone. His staff was incredible, the support of the administration and city officials, teachers, students and athletes had pulled together and reached a pinnacle. I like to think the band was a big part also, playing music, cheering and screaming, drummers drumming and the Star Spangled Girls dancing. Hurrah for Homewood.

On a personal note, I'd like to tell you the rest of the story. My Momma wasn't happy that I made the dance line. She thought dancing girls grew up to work at Sammy's. She came to meet Mrs. Wade and offered to help with our costumes. She really wanted to find a reason to pull me off the line and she was looking for the opportunity. Something happened to my mother. It wasn't long before Momma realized Mrs. Wade didn't know much about sewing and fabric selection so Momma was off and running to Hancock Fabrics and Mrs. Wade realized she had a real jewel in Momma.

She held a sewing clinic in the Home Ec room and taught all the Star Spangled Girls to sew their own pep rally outfits. She made those navy blue capes that we wore in the stands to stay warm. She made anything that Mrs. Wade asked her to and she became fast friends with that crazy girl from New Orleans. It was a friendship that lasted forty-six years. Momma worked with the Star Spangled Girls for four years until I graduated.

My little brother Keith started in the band his junior year and Momma switched to sewing, hemming and repairing band uniforms. Keith graduated but Momma didn't. She wasn't quite through as she made good friends with Pat Morrow and Daryl Ursery and worked with them until they left. Then she made friends with the new band Director, Ron Pence and his crazy assistant Chris Cooper. She stayed for forty-three years! I take full credit for that. If I had not tried out for cheerleader and failed, and tried out for Star Spangled Girls and succeeded... well you know the rest of the story. I never did dance at Sammy's though. Her name was Annie Laura Burton and I called her Momma. I miss her every day and so does the Homewood Band.

Go Patriots!

*HHS Band circa 1974 - Yankee Doodle*

**Tribute to the Band - Todd Foreman - Drum Major**

I know that Coach Bresler was a huge fan of the band as were his players. And they had a right to be. Like them, we worked hard to be the best at what we did. Freddie Pollard, our Julliard-trained Band Director from 1972-1976, worked closely with the coach and his staff in many overt ways such as our halftime shows and rallies. Our small, 80ish-member Marching Band provided incredibly entertaining shows every Friday night, including this author doing back flips (as the Drum Major), never scoring less than "superior ratings" in all competitions, marching and in-concert. Other key leaders within the band included the studious Allan Huffman as the Band Captain, tiny but tenacious Inri Tan and hard-driving Loretta Burton and as Star Spangled Girls' (SSG) Captains with Louisa Smith in-waiting, Jenise Harris as the Head Majorette, Candy King as Color

Guard Captain; Barbara Terry as Chief of the Flag Corps while Jennifer Packer served as Head of our Rifles.

Our instrument-playing Seniors that year were Al Dampier, Robin Adams, Norman Brown, John White, Alan Meacham, Sherry Trammell, Steve Zassoda, Tommy Chappell and the beloved "Class of '75 Friendliest", (Big) Mike Mitchell. Senior Majorettes: Jenise Harris, Amy Smith, and Julia West. Seniors SSG's were Shirley Slimp and Dana Smith.

Our parent support staff was great, but none more dedicated than Mrs. Annie Laura Burton, who served as the band's seamstress, logistician, taxi service, medic and "go-to-girl" for anything and everything. Any mention of the history of Homewood's Band is incomplete without her name; for forty-three years, from 1970-2013, she freely gave her time and talent. Her husband, Gene and son Keith, often pitched in, volunteering to build the mobile field podium that proved to be stable enough for me to execute fourteen dangerous back-flips off of during the extended championship season's halftime shows.

Football is a brutal sport in Alabama, always has been... especially in T-Town, Tuscaloosa that is. When temperatures rise, even the band has to play D-fense. Midway in the '73 season we played Holt High School on their home turf in Tuscaloosa. After putting a good whoopin' on 'em, the band boarded the buses in a lot outside the stadium, full of angry Holt fans. As we pulled out, the Blue-Bird was bombarded with large rocks, shattering a window, sending glass into the eyes of Majorettes Mae Johnson and Amy Smith. Standing in the aisle right next to them, I did my best to keep them from rubbing their eyes while directing the driver straight to the Emergency Room at Druid City Hospital.

Another trip to the Emergency Room occurred the following year in '74. The Band competed that year in the Fort Walton Marching Band Festival. The evening before our competition, a few of us went for a quick dip in the warm, but turbulent waters of the Florida Gulf. A younger band member was knocked unconscious by a rogue wave. Fortunately, Big Mike saw him floating, face-down about 30 yards off-shore. Not only was Mike "big and friendly"-- he was also smart, strong and quick, running like a "safety" to pull James from the foamy waters. I watched Big Mike throw that lifeless body over his shoulder like a rag-doll, and within seconds, he was on dry land performing CPR on James, saving his life. Who thought being in the band would be a dangerous undertaking? Like our football family, we had a few "close calls" of our own.

That same season, when Coach Bresler and his Pats won and won and won... I recall as vividly as if it were just the week before last. It was a long year of football games AND halftime shows. Just like our tired team of tyrants, for those of us wearing Patriot uniforms complete with blue tri-cornered hats, we were also tired...of doing the same half-time show over and over again. We could do it in our sleep. For me it was yet another opportunity to screw up a trumpet solo of "Amazing Grace" on the field. With the temperature in the 30's, as the Drum Major not having warmed up or played a note, bringing that cold metal mouthpiece to my lips was a bit scary as I wasn't ever sure what was going to come out the other end.

No complaints... I was truly honored to lead my musical magicians on the field of competition and exhibition, just as Murray Legg led his marauders. All the fans, families and friends sitting on the cold aluminum bleachers, often under blankets during that 1974 season, indeed got their money's worth... a preview to the State Championship and one of the band's greatest shows.

As soon as the team was tucked away in the locker room to strategize their coming victories, the announcer's voice boomed over the loud-speakers, "Mr. Drum Major, you may now take the field for exhibition." The band blossomed from the corner of the field with a rendition of the southern savory "Sewanee," then came to a stand-still to allow the SSG's to strut their stuff to "Chattanooga Choo." I can see them in my mind today, twenty-two arms rotating in perfect unison just like the wheels of a steam locomotive.

After "Chattanooga," came the unforgettable "Amazing Grace." Who could forget Big Mike (Mitchell) playing tuba solo. Yes, have you ever heard of a tuba solo? After getting a standing ovation for that almost every time, we then performed a circle drill to "Yankee Doodle," Tommy Hart playing solo, finishing our fifteen-minute show with another Patriot's tune, "American's We." That show won the band, our auxiliary units and the Star Spangled Girls three "Superior" ratings that year.

Of all the faculty, it was Mrs. Wade that I had the honor of working with most closely, especially during my three years as Drum Major. Shortly after her emergence from the swamps of Louisiana, Cindy Wade landed her first dance/choreography gig at nearby Shades Valley High School. Shortly thereafter, in 1972 she was not recruited, but "stolen" by both Dr. Virgil Nunn, and Michael Gross. It didn't hurt that she taught Mayor Waldrop's two daughters at Shades Valley. In her own words "I didn't even apply to teach because I loved my job at SVHS". Thankfully for our entire village, she accepted the challenge and became a PE teacher, dance instructor and gymnastics coach.

But to start her first dance line Mrs. Wade brought four "Mountiettes" with her. Captains Trisha Lawrence and Tricia Gentle, JoAnna Harding and "Bugsy" Rives. It was the Spring of 1972 and these four, along with eighteen newly-selected dancers were not yet Star-Spangled Girls, as there was no-such thing... they had not yet been named. It was up to them to decide what they wanted to be called. All the girls had a vote. In keeping with the Colonial Patriot theme, it came down to two choices, the "Starlettes" and the "Star-Spangled Girls." According to Cindy, "the girls were deadlocked between the two names. Michael Gross would be the tie-breaker, making the final decision. Instantly, he loved the sound of that most unusual title." Like many in our early days a tradition was created, the Star-Spangled Girls were born. Stars they were and stars they wore. "I wanted these ladies to look sharp and nothing less than sequins and tall white boots would do."

Alvin Bresler and Cindy Wade, both in their early 20's and both with something to prove, were much alike. Driven and disciplined, one as a Head Coach, the other as an Instructor of the Star-Spangled Girls, they would similarly tear down their athletes physically and mentally, then in short-order rebuild each one, according to their own individual strengths and weaknesses to achieve unparalleled team successes.

But no success story comes without a few bumps in the road. Cindy stated that because they were both "stubborn and determined and often having to share facilities inside and outside, that we stayed at odds with each other most of the time." However, over time as each proved their mettle on the field of competition, they gained a deep and mutual respect for one another that would manifest itself four years after Coach Bresler had left his mark on Homewood. At a Business League meeting with Cindy and Buddy present, Alvin told a group of businessmen that Cindy was the best dance coach and that her Star-Spangled Girls were the best dance team in the state. Cindy returned the favor, publicly praising him.

Cindy stated, "I always knew Alvin was a miraculous Coach, but I finally realized he had noticed that I was pretty good at what I did too. When such an accomplished male athlete notices that you and your girls' team of performers are really good, then you have arrived."

Cindy's reach is far greater than she probably could have ever imagined. In my opinion, she is at the top of the list of teachers or coaches in the history of HHS who has had such a positive influence on multiple generations of young adults in our community. After twenty-six years of serving at Homewood, Cindy retired in 1998 to join her son Billy in Real Estate. Before doing so, she ensured her legacy by replacing herself with Jennifer Meador Ayers (HHS, 1991). The last thing Cindy shared with me was this,

"I never knew teaching-love like the love I developed at Homewood High. Now, when I hear praise for the football team, the band and the Star-Spangled Girls, it makes me beam with Homewood Pride."

Unlike the very popular Star-Spangled Girls, at that time most of the other band members were often considered "geeks" but not by other bands in the state; they feared us just as Hueytown and Anniston feared our team. Though uncanny for that time, I can easily state that the band and the team shared a mutual respect that I believe still stands. We started a tradition… "working together and winning together"!

A quick note about our Alma Mater and Fight Song, "Hoorah for Homewood." Around 1970, a year or so before our dream school became a reality, we the student-body, now at HJHS, got to vote on our mascot. There were many options, but with the coming of America's 200th Bi-Centennial celebration in 1976, the red, white, and blue New England-style Patriot was an easy choice. But there was no vote for an Alma Mater or "Fight Song." Mr. Gerald Kimes, our kind, professional and meticulous Band Director at the Junior High, decided that there was no need to have separate renditions, and so the "Homewood Indian" Songs quickly became adopted as the Patriot Songs. To the freshman and sophomores (Class of '75), it made perfect sense as we had spent our first semesters stuck at the Junior High awaiting our grand entrance to HHS. It was so crowded that we attended some of our classes at Dawson Memorial Baptist Church. When it was time to change classes, a little old lady sitting in a little old chair in the hallway, would ring a little old bell. Thus, to half of the high school population, we were Patriots in Indian Territory.

Lastly, having been a cheerleader at the University of Alabama and at West Point, I'd be remiss to not mention our talented gang of rabble-rousers who spent every free moment outside of class providing essential support to their macho-men. Led by Head Cheerleader Lynda Hewlett, Seniors Ann Gurley, Dorothy Tsimpides, Debbie Tompkins, and

Melinda McDaniel, along with Juniors Dale Ramp, Linda Hallerman, Lee Anne Mathews, Virginia Ware and Helen Anderson, the cheerleaders fomented the fervor of fanatic fans through community events, games and unending pep-rallies, where Coach Bresler would always wear his custom-tailored khaki shorts and white-knit Patriots' shirt while giving his "motivational speeches". He always presented himself as the noble image of a leader; handsome, winsome, well-fit and well-spoken.

## A Tribute to our Village

This tribute is indeed meant to honor Coach Bresler. It is not complete without including many of the people who provided the stage that made it possible for him and his teams to perform their pigskin magic, paving the way for many future champions. That stage is the City of Homewood, and there is a substantial supporting cast.

I was proud to have had both personal and professional relationships with a few of our "founding-fathers," especially Mayor Bob Waldrop. He was special... more of a mentor/uncle figure than a politician. On numerous occasions, even on Saturdays, I would ride my bike 2-3 blocks from my house on Poinciana to his office. I was there so often that his secretary, Mrs. Scruggs, would eventually just let me walk-into his office unannounced. He always welcomed me and he never seemed rushed as we spent time talking about the new high school, or strategizing about how he was going to help get me into West Point (which he did), but mostly about its up-and-coming football team.

The summer before going off to the US Military Academy, I wanted to get in Rocky Balboa shape and asked "Mayor Bob" for a job with the city, cutting grass, digging ditches... he-man kind of stuff. At 0-dark-thirty the next week, I reported to the city's motor-pool at the curve on Central Ave. I was quickly directed to "get my ass" up on the back of a garbage truck. After making a few stops in Rosedale to pick up the remaining crew, I suffered the rest of the day's heat retrieving those now-antique 40-pound, corrugated steel garbage cans (full of trash) from the back yards of some of my bewildered best buddies (as they watched from their kitchen windows). I can honestly say that the first job I ever had was as a "garbage man"... but thankfully it would only last for one day. After work that day, I went once again to Mayor Waldrop's office and told him that though I was grateful for the job and the $2.30/hour it brought, that I preferred to be on the "Streets" side of the "Streets and Sanitation Department." He was furious and immediately called the Manager, demanding that I not ride the butt-end of a dump truck ever again. I ask you, what Mayor today allows a teenager to hang out in his office, and helps him get a job, and go to college?

Mayor Bob's City Council was also a critical player in the "making of magic" of our nascent high school, in the winning of our first Championship Ring, the five to follow and every accomplishment since. In 1974, the Councilmen were (Secretary) Cassie Miller, Mr. Charles Sutton, Claiborne Seier, John Parker, Roy Maguire, Harrison Lloyd, Dal Haltiwanger, R. L. Grantham, Melvin Forrester, Arthur M. Fix, Jr. and Mr. Afton Lee, a first.

Mr. Fix was the father of one of my closest friends, Art Maddox "the 3rd," who played a mean saxophone in the band and, among many accomplishments, was the Editor of our Annual, the Heritage. Much like many other dads and moms in our kind community, his kind parent was a servant at heart... in his church, in our school, and in the community, not only on the City Council, but serving as a Scout Master and Leader on the Birmingham Area Council of Boy Scouts for many years.

Another first, our Superintendent of Education was Dr. Virgil Nunn, whose bright and beautiful daughter, Joy, taught me and many others at HHS. His team included Dr. George French, Dr. Hugh Bailey, James Holloway, Richard Owens, Horace Parker, Robert Blackshear, and Mamie Foster, the sole woman on the Board of Education.

Both the City Council and the Board of Education were all generational Homewoodians whose children became our schoolmates and good friends to this day. They gladly volunteered their time and treasures to ensure that their children and their children, and theirs had better opportunities for upward mobility than they had. Is this not the "Great American Dream"? That hard-fought dream is given to us current "Homewoodians" to honor. I try to do my best to honor them, and hope that you do too, as these blessings are not meant to be taken for granted.

**A Special Tribute**

There is a significant portion of Homewood history that may be unknown, unrecognized, and even unwanted by some, that helps to explain why Homewood and indeed its fantastic football squad were the champions they were and are.

Most of Homewood's students, including me, grew up in the affluent "Leave-it-to-Beaver" neighborhoods of Hollywood, Edgewood, and Oak Grove. If you recall the abbreviated history lesson, nearly one hundred years ago, "Rosedale Park" was the first to join with Edgewood to become the City of Homewood. It was years later that Hollywood and Oak Grove joined in. Rosedale was Homewood before Homewood was Homewood. But it seems that this historic Homewood neighborhood was not included in the continued upward economic development that all of its other neighborhoods enjoyed. As Homewood's road infrastructure expanded, about the time that the new high school was being conceived, Rosedale shrunk from its original 110 acres to less than 30.

Any discussion of the history of Rosedale is not complete without the telling of the story of aforementioned Mr. Afton Lee. Though Coach Bresler's first was a great first, there were other firsts that came, well... first.

Afton Lee was the first and only African-American on our Council at that time. His son, Mike, was a fellow trumpet-player in the band with me. During the 1974 football season, I made several visits to Rosedale to visit

Mr. Lee's Grocery next to the Homewood Barber Shop. It was a two-story brownstone in which Afton had grown up. He was gentle and unassuming, one of the most humble men I have ever met. In addition to being a City Councilman, he was also Vice President of Birmingham's black-owned Citizens Federal Savings and Loan. His father, Damon Lee, one of the original landowners in Rosedale, had opened that store around 1909, long before Homewood was incorporated. Damon, born in 1870 to former slaves, with only a 4th grade education, could never have conceived that he and his descendants would help create such a dream: access, for all, to the best academic, athletic and extracurricular programs known to the State of Alabama.

Under the guidance of dedicated visionaries like Afton Lee, there were other firsts, such as Mrs. Mamie Foster, Homewood's first woman and African-American Board of Education member (and a huge Fighting Patriots fan). Along with these first officially appointed and elected civil-servants, the African-American citizens of Rosedale, played a huge role in the development of our quintessential Norman Rockwell village, and even more importantly, in the development of our burgeoning young minds.

Dr. Martin Luther King's life-giving efforts to integrate all schools, along with the closure of Rosedale High School in 1969, brought to Homewood's Elementary Schools, the Junior High and subsequently Homewood High some of its best students, including 3 super-athletes on Coach Bresler's 1974 championship team: Herman Maxwell (Seadog), #80, a starter at defensive end, Bobby Shearer (Hamp), #76, defensive tackle and "most improved player" of the season. Last, but not least, Jimmy Lee Edwards (Scoop), a running back with explosive speed whose last touchdown provided Homewood with its first State Championship Trophy.

It also brought to Homewood High some superb and inspirational teachers; too many to mention, but I must say that the brilliant and indomitable Mrs. Patricia Tolbert was the first woman of color that I came to know and love and deeply respect. Along with Michael Gross and Coach Clayton, she too encouraged me (even though my calculus skills were wanting) to attend West Point Military Academy, where I graduated and served as an Infantry Officer in the US Army in both war and in peace. There was the gentle and genteel Mr. Robert Thomas, the crazily unpredictable Mr. Hawkins, the ever-so-gracious Mamie Webber, the humble, soft-spoken Evelyn Levert, the brainy Mr. Dedrick. For those of you who didn't get to know those in our lunchroom and custodial staff under the watchful eyes of Mrs. Moses and Lawley - like Herman Reese, Floyd Gates and Mamie Harris, well you just missed out on meeting some beautiful people!

Having spent much of my childhood in Possum Town, Mississippi and then in the North Birmingham community of Norwood, all in my comfortable little white-world, these fellow students and nurturing teachers of African-American descent opened my squinted eyes and often closed mind to the value and necessity of inclusion and diversity in education, in the workplace, and in the community. They all made Homewood and its school system better, and gave us athletes that without, we may well have not been the champions that we became and remain today.

## In Closing

Together, just like Coach Bresler and his tenacious team, all of us Homewood folks, black, white, and brown contributed as best as we were able, in our own unique ways, to make Homewood, its schools, churches, businesses, parks and cozy homes, the best place in America... maybe even in the whole world, to praise our God, fly our flags and raise our families.

As I like to say, "there's no ham like Birmingham and no home like Homewood".

God Bless You and Keep You..........Todd

## Conclusion by Patrick Kirk

It was February 4th, 2020 when I met with Alvin for one of the last interviews for this book. He related to me the times he rode to Homewood basketball games with my Dad and Mom and the enjoyment he had talking sports and business stuff with Lyle Kirkpatrick, as he called him. Dad later told me of the relationship these two had and the discussions they had about our team and the potential for calling my number on third downs. As an adult, Dad told me what Alvin did to get me more prominently into the offense. Once I proved myself in the open field others called my number in third and long situations and I delivered. These are the things of parents and their children.

As Coach Bresler and I talked over lunch and I told him some stories he didn't know or remember (why should he? it's been forty-five years, at least), it dawned on me it was my Dad's birthday and he would have been 92, and here I am remembering him as I write this book about those precious years we still cherish. I have been reminded by friends that know me as well as I know myself that as much as Dad and I butted heads on Shades Park Drive and at the meat plant during my teen years and even into my twenties, Dad had my best interests at heart and I would have been well served to listen to him, which of course I didn't.

My son reminds me that the man he called Papi had a good heart and he remembers the large strong hands that held him so tight at the rides at Disneyland, just as I remember my grandfather's steel worker hands holding me as I steered his Ford tractor in the fields of Shelby County as a six year old. And so it goes, my wrinkled hands hold my two month old granddaughter on Friday mornings as this Papi babysits her and plays his '70's music to keep her calm after a bottle. Emma has many great days ahead and I hope she has a grade school and high school experience like I had at Homewood. We were very lucky by any standard and so many leaders such as Alvin Bresler put us first and taught us the meaning of hard work and high standards.

For me personally it was men like Nick O'Grady, Riley Harmon, Michael Gross, David Beason, David Jones, Jackie Clayton, Wayne Sheets and Alvin Bresler that had such an impact on this adolescent and teen that I was able to overcome the angst and rancor and somehow achieve beyond my reach. They all experienced first-hand the episodes of behavior that must have exasperated them beyond all expectations, only to somehow keep me between the rails deemed acceptable. I owe them a debt of gratitude that I cannot repay as much as I might try. So I will simply say thank you and I love you all. And that message I send to heaven to my Dad more than ever here in my 63rd year on this earth.

*Patrick Kirk - Researching in Peru*

My Mom is still with us playing the organ at eighty-nine and swimming three times a week in better shape than all her children combined. Thanks Mom for all the help and understanding as I tried your patience more than any other. She recently read my first book and will enjoy this one even more as she is a Fighting Patriot through and through. And to Mom, my siblings and friends who endured the loss of a daughter-in-law, sister-in-law, and close friend, my wife Tracy in 2001 and helped raise her boy as if he were their own, I have no words that can aptly relate our gratitude.

Finally, to my teammates who experienced the love and camaraderie afforded us by those mentioned herein and many other leaders of Homewood, I hope this reading finds you healthy and happy, just as we were on that cold December night in 1974 when the Lord above saw fit to bless us with a lesson of championship unity, appreciation and that moment of fleeting glory: "We're # 1".

Many thanks to Lisa Hodgens, Anne Hill Henders and Shawn Wright for donating their hard work out of loyalty to Homewood High School that made this book possible. If not for the thirty plus contributors to this book we would not have been able to memorialize the first three years of Homewood football with accuracy, and we hope we have made it an enjoyable read.

For those of us who played on the three teams our memories have been challenged and updated as to the facts and events that have faded. Our group has lost some members as we are all in our sixties now, but our love for them remains intact. Rest in peace Rick Powers (P), David Fleisher (Norman), Larry Riffe, David (the Marine) Dozier and Jerry Winstead.

As mentioned, any profits after expenses from the sale of this book will go to charity. We continue to support the Fighting Patriots and their march to more championships for Homewood High School.

# ADDENDUM

Thirty Contributors to this book:

Murray Legg - Story & Quote

Alvin Bresler - Offense, Defense & Quotes

Bill Holmes - Quote

Peter Braasch - Quotes

Dean Snow - Quotes

Charles Boyd - Story and Quote

Wayne Sheets - Yearbook Tribute, Story & Quote

Jimmy Glass - Story and Quote

Alan Hardin - Quote

Ray Powell - Story

Tim Calloway - Story

Wade Kirkpatrick - Story and Quotes

Roger Malcolm - Story

Skip Taylor - Story

Melinda McDaniel Leavelle - Cheerleading review 1974

Randy Smith - Story

Bob Foreman - Quote

Susan Steiner Farlow - Cheerleading review 1972

Michael Gross - Forward

Rolan "Stoney" Jackson - Story and Quotes

Chuck Yow - Story

David Beason - Offense & Quotes

Dave Jones - Quotes

Mark Robbins - Story and Quotes

Joe Wurtele - Story

Herman Maxwell - Story

Todd Foreman - Introduction, Band and other Tributes

Loretta Burton - Star-Spangled Girls review

Cindy Wade - Star-Spangled Girls Quotes

Shawn Wright - Story and Cover Design

Anne Hill Henders - Editing

Lisa Hodgens - Final Editing

Made in USA - Kendallville, IN
1083169_9781098305178
04.21.2020 1218